Islam among Urban Blacks

Muslims in Newark, New Jersey: A Social History

Michael Nash

UNIVERSITY PRESS OF AMERICA,® INC.
Lanham • Boulder • New York • Toronto • Plymouth, UK

Copyright © 2008 by
University Press of America,® Inc.
4501 Forbes Boulevard
Suite 200
Lanham, Maryland 20706
UPA Acquisitions Department (301) 459-3366

Estover Road
Plymouth PL6 7PY
United Kingdom

Library of Congress Control Number: 2007933968
ISBN-13: 978-0-7618-3865-4 (clothbound : alk. paper)
ISBN-10: 0-7618-3865-1 (clothbound : alk. paper)
ISBN-13: 978-0-7618-3866-1 (paperback : alk. paper)
ISBN-10: 0-7618-3866-X (paperback : alk. paper)

To the pioneers . . . the foundation builders

Contents

Foreword

A city always belongs more to the past than to the present, even as its inhabitants professing the ideal of progress try to modernize it.

—Fernando Marias

Islam Among Urban Blacks: A Social History of Muslims in Newark NJ, describes the life story about the emergence of Islam in Newark, NJ, which gives rise to a discourse in relation to religious belief, religious practice, ethnic identity and the altering of ancestral relationships. It is easy to forget what Roger Scruton has told us: "there are two types of distinct phenomena involved in religion, as we know it: religious observance and religious belief, which do not necessarily coincide." The chapters of this ethnography carefully sketch the story of the often-overlooked social history of 'urban Islam' and specifically the intervention of a number of religious protagonists who interrogate a type of trans-ethnic/pan-Islamic practice, belief and indigenous identity. In this exchange from the early 20th century to the present day there has been bouts of orthodox Islam, religious decay (*al-inhitat*), intellectual skepticism and arguments from self-proclaimed prophets that are openly blasphemous.

In the post 9-11 world names and place of origin are still meaningful although politicized; in the 20th century, in the city of Newark, the host community, the theological movement of the 'religious' protagonist was pregnant with a reform agenda but they were nevertheless faced with the transformation, adaptation and the presence of Islam and Muslims. In this *Weltanschauung* there is moreover a contradiction of terms; it begins with names such as 'Moorish Science Temple' and their beliefs, which evolves to orthodox Islam and the somewhat improved inheritance of a religious 'Hamitic Arab' identity by the time we get to Professor Ezaldeen. Professor Michael Nash has shared with us the importance of this discourse, and this evolution, with adequate details about each bout and each protagonist in his meta-narrative and above all the emotional impact associated with Islam, but what is most intriguing is that the reader will find that the picture is more complex. Take for instance the Chinese proverb "The beginning of wisdom is to call things by their right names"; in this sense the culture of how one defines him or herself vis-à-vis a religious doctrine is itself an argument. Furthermore as Foucault postulates, "knowledge is enmeshed in power relations", first returning to Noble Drew Ali, 'power relations' are obvious with the establishment of the Moorish Science Temple, but in these 'power relations' there are many contradiction of appearances, as his followers are apparently transported back in time. Perhaps a few members knew better, if this is the case, Professor Ezaldeen's religious curriculum could be seen as the instrument of religious revival and the willingness to live up to Islam's orthodox teachings.

There is something in this story for every student. The student of philosophy would find that the belief in 'black' prophethood, i.e., Noble Drew Ali and the rest of the self declared prophets, suggest hybridity with Nietzsche's idea that "God is the projection of man's uneasy conscience." For the student of sociology and 'Black Religion' as Professor Sherman Jackson calls it, the racializing of Moorish, Hamitic or Black is inseparable from one's religious identity and social class. Finally the student of anthropology would be puzzled over the master and member relationship, and over the rituals, which establish the bond of membership and gender relations. But above all the student of history will find it most useful for comparison within the context of social history among 'urban blacks'. In this regard the text is a marker because it helps us to understand the shared cultural experiences and the collective treatment and hierarchies of religious practices among the adherents of orthodox Muslims, proto-Islamic movements and their contenders over the last century in the city of Newark.

Twentieth century attitudes towards religion may have affected the way we view Islam and Muslims and hasty judgments are quite common in the midst of recent political concerns. Today, Islam in the city of Newark is imbedded with a transnational and highly politicized identity but place of origin is still meaningful; likewise religious practice and urban multiculturalism co-exist through institutions like the urban mosque. If this is the case, linking Nash's text *Islam Among Urban Blacks,* to the historical foundation of the city we find a specific aim: that of developing an academic apparatus with reference to the social history of Islam among urban blacks.

Akel Ismail Kahera Ph.D.

Preface

WHAT THIS STUDY IS AND IS NOT

This study is not about the Islamic religion as much as it is about the history of a people impacted by it, and it is not about a people impacted by Islam as much as it is about a culture reinvented by an American people. Some have called it a story of a work in progress. Further, it is not about one particular community. The Moorish American, African American Sunni and the Nation of Islam organizations in the context of Newark history are at the center of the discussion. I have chosen them because they were the leading groups in Newark that introduced Islamic culture to its residents and thus serve, in my judgment, as the best starting point for this discussion. The three groups mentioned above founded institutions in the city of Newark to preserve their identity. The spirit in Newark when Noble Drew Ali is believed to have arrived there in 1913 welcomed people from various parts of the country and world and from all walks of life. Indeed, Newark in the early twentieth century was described by the business gurus of the day as "the City of Opportunity." This prospect attracted many in search of a better life to Newark's thriving industrial centers. Many African-Americans from the south, during the Great Migration and before, chose Newark or "New Ark" as a place of settlement. Among those African-Americans were people who had been oriented to the Islamic religion and were quite nostalgic about having been separated from Africa and things African. Moreover, this story is about the religious and cultural expressions of a people, whose ancestral roots are from Africa, yet historically marginalized—socially, culturally, economically and politically—in a so-called free and democratic society. In many ways this story can be characterized as one about the dynamic and creative expressions of a spiritually resilient and determined people whose rediscovery of their forgotten roots have contributed to their cultural reinvention in American society. Dr. Akel Kahera, author of *Deconstructing the American Mosque: Space, Gender and Aesthetics,* has described it as a well documented study of the indigenous Muslim community in Newark.

AMERICA'S MUSLIMS: ISLAM IN THE FABRIC OF AMERICAN SOCIETY AND CULTURE

Thanks to the works of professors Allan Austin, Michael Gomez, Sylvianne Diouf, Sulayman Nyang, Abdullah Hakim-Quick and others, we now know that African Muslim slaves in America, as well as Muslim visitors to this part of the world from Africa during the pre-Columbian and antebellum periods— some of which would be deemed free men in the newly formed United States—found ways to hold on to their Islamic faith even under hostile conditions in America. We also know that somewhere along the line the relentless effort by them to maintain their Islamic identity and pass it on to their progeny was passed on to those who would carry Islamic ideals into Newark in the twentieth century. Among those who received the torch were Noble Drew Ali, Muhammad Ezaldeen and James 3X Shabazz. These teachers and representatives of distinct brands of Islam and black-nationalist ideas would carry Islamic symbols and values to people in the back alleys and streets of Newark, NJ as one observer put it. Their story is an American story about trails, tribulation, survival and triumph.

Therefore to attempt to tell this story about African Americans influenced by Islam in Newark, NJ, with all of its complexity and apparent contradictions, is indeed controversial and quite an undertaking. Be that as it may, African Americans, especially those among them who would be influenced in some way by Islam in the twentieth century, have pioneered the effort to reconstruct the African identities of the ex-slaves. The figureheads of the major organizations in Newark would work hard to restore their people's faith in the best of their ancestral traditions and community life, while at the same time encouraging them to contribute positively to the social well being of the United States—their country of birth—and to the demands of modern life, despite being in a racially fused, politically polarized and religiously hostile environment.

THE QUESTION OF IDENTITY

No doubt the task has been an arduous one, and for a number of reasons, primarily because African and African American intellectuals have not yet arrived at a consensus on how to define Africanity. When the Kenyan born American scholar Dr. Ali Mazrui[1] stated in his book, *Africanity Redefined,* that Africanity should be defined as an idea rather than as a point of origin, this provocative declaration was a challenge to the ideas of major thinkers on the subject of black identity. Among those thinkers are Dr. Molefi Asante of Temple University who popularized the term Afrocentricity, the scholar/ activist Dr. Malauna Karenga, the founder of Kwaanza, the Egyptologist Dr. Ben Jochanan, the late Dr. John Henrik Clarke and the humble and studious Dr. Leonard Jeffries of City University in New York and others. The opinions of these scholars within the last twenty-five years have become increasingly popular on the streets of urban African America, and until recently, with little competition from their Sunni Muslim colleagues in the academy. Mazrui who has distinguished himself as an important voice on the idea of Africanity as it relates to Muslims is among the Africanists whose works are largely un-known in black urban America. In my view Mazrui's definition stated above, which is rooted both in the values of African spirituality and the Traditions of Prophet Ibrahim (Abraham) has, unfortunately, had less exposure in urban African America; hence, leaving a great number of Muslim people found in those areas without intellectual and spiritual support. That is to say that Mazrui's analysis of what it means to be African, (which differs somewhat from that of the gurus of Afrocentric thought) I believe, is a good starting point for all those (especially Muslims of African descent) who love and iden-tify in some way with Africa. Africans on the continent and throughout the Diaspora who understand the cultural and religious diversity of the African continent, the depth of African spirituality and the mandates of the principles of modern statehood can certainly appreciate Mazrui's commentary and the elucidation of his perspective. Like the Afrocentrists, Mazrui tries to build a bridge between cultural and religious diversity, African spirituality and the prospects for modernization and democratization with respect to nation-building on the continent of Africa.

FREEDOM'S QUEST

However, what is of particular interest to me is that within the twentieth cen-tury Newark context all of the contradictions outlined above have in some way played themselves out among the common people who have pioneered the effort to establish Muslim community life. Thus, the Islamic experience in Newark—a microcosm of the broader experience of Muslims in other parts of the state—serves on one level as a mirror not only for the struggles of Mus-lims in New Jersey but also the entire country. The relevance of this point to my study is that the Islamic experience in America is inextricably tied to the

African American experience as Sherman A. Jackson points out in his groundbreaking, seminal, study entitled *Islam and the Blackamerica: Looking Toward the Third Resurrection*. And so the history of the Islamic influence in Newark, NJ, the foundation of which was laid by African Americans, is not a story about a people connected to those operating on the periphery of the struggle for civil and human rights; rather, it is a story about the soul and struggle of a people, an American people, despised and rejected by mainstream Euro-American society for a great part of the history of this nation. But as history progressed in the U.S., few within the dominant culture imagined that the sons and daughters of former slaves in the twentieth century would eventually rise and develop the convictions and courage to exercise their conscience and rights under the laws of the land as they struggled to reinvent themselves and articulate an alternative vision for their people and the country that they have grown to love and now call home. This vision, culminating and best articulated in the Islamically inspired teachings of the students and helpers of the American born Imam W. Deen Mohammed—the son of Clara and Elijah—in the Newark area, consisted of embracing the idea of the American Dream and the Great American Experiment insofar as these were concerned with the achievement of freedom, justice and equality for African Americans and also for all Americans and all people.

Nevertheless, this short study on Muslim history in Newark, NJ is best described as a story about the primary organizations and personalities in Newark that helped shape the multifaceted and multicultural face of Greater Newark's vibrant Muslim community. In spite of the rich diversity of expression within the Newark Islamic community, the humanistic values of the Prophet Muhammad, in many ways, were articulated by each of them. And although Islamic influences in the United States third oldest city is probably as old as the city itself, the twentieth century Islamic consciousness movement, especially within black America, gives us a foundation upon which to understand and reconstruct the lives of those men and women during the days of slavery who tried to hold on to the values of their universal faith in a hostile social system that was based not on universality, equality and inclusion but ethnocentrism, inequality and exclusion. To discriminate on the basis of ethnicity and race was an aberration to the principles of the American Revolution. Did not Thomas Jefferson say that "all men are created equal with certain inalienable rights and that among these rights are life, liberty and the pursuit of happiness." Africans who came from societies that did not systematically alienate people because of the color of their skin did not understand the ethnocentric approach to nation-building espoused by European Americans. Secondly, inequality in African societies did not exist as a result of some alleged physical or mental incapacity of entire groups of people, nor were entire groups of people excluded by law from enjoining in the natural rights to freedom. Therefore Africans, whether they were Christians, Muslims or adherents of the Traditional religions, found the ethnocentrism of the European Americans to be very distasteful. Nevertheless, they had to, and did, find ways to survive and live within this very hostile social milieu; but they were deprived culturally. Many of them, in their identification with the struggle for freedom of the American colonists against the British, experienced a paradigm shift by latching on to the ideas of the European Enlightenment. Some examples are the astute West African turned poet, Phyllis Wheatley, and the scientist Benjamin Banneker who played a major role in the design of Washington D.C. Other enslaved Africans, not so well known, resisted adopting the ways and attitudes of European Americans and instead struggled to maintain their African/Islamic value system that had served their people for centuries. Some good examples are the Prince among Slaves, Abdur Rahman and Job Ben Solomon. Though these men were not successful in establishing thriving Muslim communities within the American slave system, their efforts to resist Euro-American religious indoctrination are well documented. Other examples of resistance involve those Africans that somehow got entangled within the American slave system but felt a strong connection to one of the United States' long time allies, Morocco. In 1776, the sultan of Morocco established a treaty with the thirteen colonies which stated that subjects of Morocco could not be enslaved like other Africans. There has always been a community of Africans, knowledgeable about this agreement, who have felt it to be binding on the United States to honor its historical significance and sacredness. Because Morocco was and still is a Muslim country, a close examination of this history and the Americans who feel connected to it, can help us to better understand the influence of Islam not only in Newark where Noble Drew Ali began organizing and educating the public about it, but also in the whole of the United States of America, a place that accepted help from Muslims, but denied their right to live as first-class citizens in the New American Republic built in the name of liberty and freedom.

NOTE

1. Ali Mazrui is also the author of *The Africans: a Triple Heritage*. This important book, published in 1986 by Little, Brown and Company, is a must read. It is the companion volume to the acclaimed PBS Series, "The Africans."

Acknowledgments

I am one of Newark, New Jersey's native sons. Born and raised in this ever-evolving city, I have had the opportunity to experience, first hand, the dynamism of its diverse peoples and its urban culture. As my memory serves me, it was in this city that I first made contact with the universal religion of al-Islam. My older siblings, all of whom cherished and looked after me when I was young, either had Muslim friends that they were in regular contact with or became Muslims themselves, which contributed to my early exposure to the religion. My first cousin, Salim, took me along with his family to Florida during my middle school years. We visited a masjid (mosque) for juma'ah (Friday prayer) there and the mental image of that experience, though somewhat vague, is still in my memory bank. My older siblings, Bobby and Richie, especially, I'm told, and Salim, would sometimes talk to the younger ones in the family about what they knew of Islam. Although the Christian sensibilities of my parents and aunt—God bless their souls—often discouraged this, the influence of Islam would apparently enter into my subconscious mind when I was young, and eventually capture my imagination beginning in my high school years, and reaching its apex in my college years. While I was a student at Rutgers University-Newark campus I decided that I would take the shahada, and began my spiritual and intellectual journey as an observant Muslim. When I graduated from Rutgers and entered graduate school, enveloped by the spirit and influenced by the works of my former professor, Dr. Clement Alexander Price, New Jersey's foremost authority on the history of the African-American community in the state, I made a decision to write about the story of a people that impacted my life and whose experience, which could not be found in any book, I became fascinated with—the Muslims in Newark, NJ.

There are many people who contributed to the completion of this book as well as to my knowledge of Muslim history in Newark. The local Muslims, in many ways, taught and nurtured me. The mosques they established became spiritual sanctuaries for me and many others. Like many people in Greater Newark I have had the opportunity to learn a great deal about al-Islam, its nature, and its history, both in the United States and other parts of the world, from hearing public lectures. As I immersed myself in the many informative books on al-Islam and Muslim history that could be found at conferences and programs I attended, beginning in my undergraduate years at Rutgers University, my thinking about my own life became transformed. The "Islam in Perspective Lecture Series" sponsored by the former Islamic Center of East Orange (ICEO) in the 1980s and 1990s; for instance, contributed to my determination to further educate myself about this often misunderstood religion and world influence. The ICEO, in conjunction with the Islamic Students Organization of Rutgers University-Newark, brought in a number of Muslim educators and scholars to share information publicly about Islam and the Muslim peoples throughout the world. It was a very enlightening lecture series. I also remember attending in the late 1980s a very insightful lecture at the Meadowlands Arena titled "Sacred Life Connections." The event was sponsored by the historic Masjid Mohammed-Newark (now Masjid Ali Muslim), and the keynote speaker was the current leader of the Mosque Cares Association, Imam W. Deen Mohammed, the son of Clara and Elijah. Imam W. Deen's social and political philosophy, articulated over the years since 1975, upon investigation, struck me as profound and consistent with Islamic principles as well as the freedom-loving and democratic spirit of the American people.

This particular work began in 1993 as my master's thesis in history for the School of History, Political Science and International Studies at Farleigh Dickinson University (FDU). The dedicated members of the graduate history faculty there prepared its students for an enriching global experience in the study of history and world affairs. I studied with people from many parts of the world, and was enriched in the process.

I would like to thank and salute FDU's Dr. Helen Brudner, director of the graduate program and Dr. Faramarz Fatemi, the department chair, for giving me the freedom, encouragement, and support to pursue my interest in the study of Muslim-American history as a graduate student. The excellent training I received at FDU prepared me for the challenges I would face in writing this book. While there are books written about other ethnic and religious communities in the state of New Jersey that can easily be found on library shelves, not one by any academician has been written about the many Muslims that share space with other people in the state. This reality, in part, inspired me to write this book. Hence, this work is an important introduction to the subject of Muslim history in NJ. My examination of some primary and secondary sources, as well as interviews conducted with many of the pioneers, has made it possible to reconstruct, to some degree, the history of the Newark Muslim community. It was indeed a monumental task yet a rewarding experience. FDU's Dr. Kalman Goldstein and Dr. Barbara Horan, especially, did meticulous grading of my graduate school papers which contributed much to my development as a thinker and a writer, and my ability to complete this task with confidence. Thank you.

There are others whose friendship and intellect served as an indispensable and constant source of strength and inspiration to me as I was writing this book. My dear friends, Rodney McNeil (The Poet) and Ronald Strothers, also a poet and gifted novelist, were always encouraging and reflective when I came to them with a problem. They could always be counted on to be true and honest as conscience demands. I was often energized after our friendly discussions on matters of life and what sometimes turned out to be intellectual sparring sessions; and, more often than not, walked away with a renewed spirit and clearer sense of self and purpose.

There are so many others to thank. Historian and scholar Dr. Clement Alexander Price of Rutgers University believed in me from the very beginning of my journey to the study of Muslim history among African-Americans in the United States. Thank you, Dr. Price, for that. I would also like to thank Giles Wright, Director of the Afro-American Studies Program at the New Jersey Historical Commission, for his well-wishes and encouragement. The work of Clement Price and Giles Wright concerning the history of the African-American community in the Garden State is our model of excellence in scholarship, as well as an inspiration to, and blueprint for my generation. I urge aspiring historians to build on the foundation that they have laid. It gives me a warm feeling inside to also remember two other extraordinary personalities in the Department of African American and African Studies at Rutgers-Newark; two men who positively impacted my life and my ability to take on and complete this work—Dr. Wendell Holbrook and Dr. Said Samatar (Uncle Said). Both men mentored me in a course or two when I was an undergraduate and didn't hesitate to apply a method of tough love when the situation I created called for it. Thank you for your patience. I am also thankful to Dr. Sulayman S. Nyang, Professor of Political Science and African Studies at Howard University, whose lectures, books and articles on the Islamic experience in America has enriched me personally and professionally. Thank you, Dr. Nyang, for sharing your knowledge and engaging our minds. Your work, too, is a model of excellence in scholarship and a blueprint for those of us in the field of Muslim-American history and studies. I thank Dr. Akbar Muhammad of Binghamton

University who gave a timely and heartfelt response to my letters and telephone calls during the time that I was gathering my information for this study. At my request, Dr. Muhammad sent me articles he had written on Muslim history and some personal thoughts about Ibn Khaldun, the 14th century Afro-Arab Muslim scholar. His letter, upon receipt, was a great source of encouragement to me. Prof. Robert (Bob) Thurston of New Jersey City University read the text in its infancy, as well as other articles I had written on the subject of Muslim-Americans, and made helpful suggestions for their improvement. Thank you, Bob, for lending your editorial skills to this effort. I would like to also acknowledge and thank the *Muslim Journal* staff, and its editor, Ms. Ayesha K. Mustafa, for publishing my articles on Newark Muslim history and also the staff at the Newark Public Library for its public display of the Dorer Collection, which included a couple of rare photographs of the Moorish-Americans in Newark. Hasim Ihsan, director and producer of "Understanding Islam," was also helpful in getting my research some early exposure through two televised interviews conducted by him in the late 1990s. Dr. Akel Kahera, a pioneer on many fronts, formally introduced my research to the academic world and inspired my interest in the history of the urban mosque in Newark. Thank you, Dr. Kahera, for returning and accepting my phone calls, even at odd hours. Dr. Lenworth Gunther, a mentor and friend and Dr. Bahir Kamil of ECC, was instrumental in the success of "Roots and Branches: A History of Muslims in the Greater Newark, NJ Community," which took place the evening of February 25, 2004 at ECC's J. Harry Smith Auditorium." Their involvement in this important community forum, the first of its kind in the state of New Jersey, helped to link the importance of my research not only to the Greater Newark Muslim community, but also to the public discourse related to the nature of struggle in our society to achieve freedom, justice and equality for all. At this forum, the institutional development of Islam in Newark and its nearby communities were discussed. Thank you, Bahir, for moderating the panel, and Lenny for convening the historic event. Also, Dr. Lenworth Gunther, Dr. Mark Schuman, Professor David Berry, Professor Isa Maack, Professor Judith Ward, Dr. Ned Wilson and Professor Gene Lieber, all of ECC, as a team made enormous contributions to my growth, development and advancement in the field of history. Without their guidance, encouragement, support and well-wishes, my first four years as a full-time member of the history faculty at ECC would have been less fruitful and more difficult. I would also like to acknowledge my colleague and friend, Eileen De Freece, who always offered good professional advice and an encouraging word for me. A special recognition goes to Ned Wilson. Ned, at my request, read the manuscript in record time as I was preparing the final draft for the publisher, and made helpful suggestions for its improvement. Thank you, Ned. And, last but not least, ECC's President Dr. A. Zachary Yamba would on occasion share with me, quite discreetly, thought provoking articles about Islam in Africa and other parts of the world. I chose to interpret these subtle gestures as evidence for my claim that he has, over the years, been a most effective educational leader who respects, encourages, and values diversity, creativity, and those committed to educational excellence. Thank you, Dr. Yamba, for the spirit you bring to educational excellence and leadership in higher education, which in some sense supported my research efforts.

I would also like to thank the elders for allowing me to speak and those pioneers and individuals who graciously shared their experiences, insights, and perspectives concerning the history of Islam in Newark, New Jersey. This book could not have been possible without the testimonies of the pioneers. There are many who shared information with me; some are mentioned by name in this book. Most helpful were Kenneth Hall (Dawud), Ahmed Burhani, Mark Bashir, Wahab Arbubakar, Malik Arbubakar, Musa Hamad, Jamallah Muhammad, Rasul Ansari, the late Imam Muhammad Armiya NuMan, the late Yusef Shakoor, Imam Wahy Deen Shareef, Imam Abdul Kareem Muhammad, Rashad El-Amin, Tariq Rahim, Earl Siddique, Imam Abdul-Aleem Razaqq, Mujiba Razaqq, the late Khalid Ismail, Matina Ismail, Khalida Haqq, Abdul Wali, Kareemah Wadud, Imam Heshaam Jaaber, James Mendheim Bey, Ahmed Batemon, Abdul Q. Muhammad, Jesse El, Dr. Abdul Salaam and many others.

To my beloved wife Valley (Nadira), and our precious daughter Sunah, the project is finally done. Thank you both for your faith, love, unyielding assistance, and patience, all of which sustained me. Allah, the Almighty, gave me a treasure in you.

It is my sincere hope that this short book will be illuminating and helpful to all those who read it, and that the members and former-members of the communities discussed therein will find it to be a fair and accurate survey of how Islam evolved among urban blacks in Newark, New Jersey. By no stretch of the imagination is this work exhaustive; rather, it should be viewed as simply a stepping stone in an unexplored direction. If you, the reader, have developed a clearer understanding of the role Islam has played in influencing a significant number of native born Americans from Newark, and the complexity of Islamic life in the United States, then I can feel confident in saying to myself that I have made a small contribution to our understanding of this neglected, yet important, part of American social and religious history. If I have failed to communicate an accurate relationship between Islam and the African American experience within the context of Newark history, then I am the only one to blame.

Introduction

To African Americans, there was little to be gained from religious opposition to Al-Islam; and since they had no real political stake in America, political opposition to the Muslim world was unworthy of serious consideration. On the contrary, African Americans early adopted the view that they were bound to the colonized people of Africa and Asia by the link of Western oppression of non-white peoples. No doubt, Egyptians were considered highly, due to the many Biblical references to their country, its geographical location in Africa, and the fact that cultural advancements predate Western civilization. Although Arabians are not Africans, the fact that they are non-white and have a history of cultural connections with Africa gave them a special place in the ideological thought of African Americans.[1]

Islamic culture and symbolism has had a traceable influence in Newark, New Jersey since 1913, the year that Timothy Drew, a migrant from North Carolina, established what many believe to be the first documented Moorish American community in the United States of America. Drew, who later changed his name to Noble Drew Ali, was followed in 1941 by Muhammad Ezaldeen, progenitor of the Hamitic (Black) Arab identification for African Americans, who established a chapter of the Addeynu Allahe Universal Arabic Association (AAUAA) at 95 Prince Street, Newark, New Jersey. This organization gave birth to a number of Sunni Muslim groups. Baitul Quraish (the House of Quraish), a leading Sunni Muslim organization that was very active in the city of Newark during the late 1960s up until the mid 1970s is perhaps the most significant. There were others, such as Masjid Deenul-Lah founded by Hajj Akeel Karam and the Jehadi Institute founded by the late Hajj Heshaam Jaaber who received national acclaim when he performed the *janaza* (funeral) prayer of Hajj Malik El-Shabazz, better known as Malcolm X. Although this organization had its base in Elizabeth, New Jersey, it had a lot of influence among Muslims in Newark. All of these organizations were headed by and composed of African Americans.

Juxtaposed with these developments was the experience of African Americans who were members of the Nation of Islam, perhaps the greatest black-nationalist Muslim organization this country has ever seen. With the establishment in 1959 of the Temple #25 first on Camden Street and then on South Orange Avenue by Minister James 3X Shabazz, the Nation of Islam began to make its presence felt in the city of Newark. In 1973 James was murdered in Newark and by 1975 Elijah Muhammad, the spiritual guide of the NOI national body had died. Upon succeeding his father in 1975 as the Nation of Islam's new spiritual guide, Wallace D. Muhammad began to gradually introduce the members of the NOI organization to new concepts that were consistent with mainstream Islamic thought. This was a new beginning for the NOI people nation-wide. The concepts he introduced according to one of the Newark faithful brought some confusion in Newark because people in the NOI, while under Elijah, had never heard some of the things he told them. As a result, there was a power struggle between those who wanted to see the NOI evolve into the world community of Islam as proposed by the new chief minister, Wallace Deen Muhammad, those who wanted to revive the old teachings of Elijah Muhammad, and those who were not sure which direction and at what pace the organization should move. The inability to agree on the direction that the Newark chapter of the NOI would take and the pace at which it would move by Hussein Shabazz, the resident Imam, and Ahmed Burhani, a former Arabic Instructor for the University of Islam and assistant to Hussein, ultimately resulted in a major split in 1981. It was this year that a second new beginning was witnessed for many of the people that were a part of the Newark experience. Lead by Ahmed Burhani, formerly James 51X, several key members of the Nation of Islam, reportedly with Imam Muhammad's blessings, made a split with the historic Temple #25 on South Orange Avenue and established a new *masjid* at 237 Central avenue, East Orange, dedicated to the propagation of the new orthodox Islamic teachings as represented by chief Minister Wallace D. Muhammad. It was at this location that what eventually became the Islamic Center of East Orange under Burhani's Imamship got its beginning.[2] Burhani was instrumental in the extension of this *dawah* (Islamic propagation) effort into the East Orange area. Burhani's *hijra*[3] from the South Orange Avenue base seemed to start a chain reaction, as other prominent NOI members in subsequent years also branched off to establish new Muslim communities in other parts of the greater Newark area. Among them were the education director of the University of Islam, Abdul Kareem Muhammad, now resident Imam of Masjid Al-Haqq-Newark and Wahyudeen Shareef, a former NOI secretary and present Imam of Masjid Warithideen housed within the WARIS Cultural Research and Development Center in Irvington, NJ. These important institutions today are undoubtedly pillars of the Greater Newark Muslim community, and have been very active in the spread of ideas relative to the practice of the Islamic faith.

Hence, although there are a considerable number of foreign-born Muslims in the area now, many of whom are Egyptian, Guyanese, Palestinian, Pakistani, African, and Chinese origin, African Americans are the oldest organized group, with the largest membership. They have been in the forefront of the efforts to promote Muslim community development since the early part of the 20th century. African Americans made the sacrifices and laid the foundation for the practice of Al-Islam in the state of New Jersey. Some argue that Newark, as a result of Noble Drew Ali's influence there in the early part of this century, should always have a special place in the hearts of all Muslim Americans, for, according to historian Adib Rashad, "Noble Drew Ali was undoubtedly the first quasi-Islamic pioneer in the United States who signed the first charter making the Moorish Science Temple of America (MSTA) a legally incorporated movement."[4]

This study seeks to describe the historic and heroic role of African Americans influenced by al-Islam in Newark, New Jersey, and show how their presence and efforts, though seldom acknowledged, has not only had the greatest impact on the growth and development of a viable Islamic community in the city, but also how African American Muslims have made a significant and positive contribution to the process of social change on the urban American landscape. Indeed, the Islamic consciousness movement in African America was an overlooked, misunderstood and/or unexamined branch of the civil rights movement. Further, this study, in some sense, seeks to provide a local context in which to understand the Islamic impact in the whole of North America, described by New Jersey historian Clement Alexander Price as one of the most remarkable phenomenon of the 20th century.

NOTES

1. Akbar Muhammad, "Interaction Between Indigenous and Immigrant Muslims in the United States: Some Positive Trends," *Hijrah Magazine*, Mar/Apr. (1985): 14.

2. In 1984 members of the East Orange community established a *masjid* on Lincoln Street in East Orange, NJ. and in the mid 1990s secured a larger building on Oraton Parkway in East Orange. They have renamed their community, Masjid Ahlis Sunnah. Also, the Muslim Community Development Center of Essex County on 18th

street and 4th Avenue, East Orange evolved largely out of the efforts of other individuals who, too, were active on Lincoln Street.

3. The english translation for *hijra* is migration.

4. Adib Rashad, *Elijah Muhammad & The Ideological Foundation Of The Nation Of Islam* (Virginia: U.B. & U.S. Communication Systems, 1994), 79.

Chapter One

The Early Stages

MUSLIM FRIENDS OF THE AMERICAN REVOLUTION

The Muslims of Morocco, descendants of the Moors, were among the first friends of the American Revolution. In 1777, under the leadership of Sultan Sidi Muhammad Ben Abdullah, Morocco recognized the independence of the United States and granted free rights of passage to all American ships.[1] Alan Austin states in his book, *African Muslims in Antebellum America*, that the first treaty of the new nation was made with Morocco. When the North African Barbary States of Tripoli, Tunis, Morocco and Algiers contended with pirate ships in their territories, Morocco, after Britain and France were no longer able to protect American ships in the Mediterranean and the Atlantic, became an ally of the United States. One of the new nation's first international military adventures, on "the shores of Tripoli," North Africa, is memorialized in "The Marine's Hymn."[2] This fact of early U.S. diplomatic history, rarely mentioned or discussed in academic circles of the West, helps to recover another missing link in the twentieth century Muslim American saga.

The founder of the Moorish Science Temple of America (MSTA), Noble Drew Ali, was known for his vivid orations concerning Morocco when he addressed the African Americans who were becoming concentrated in America's northern industrialized cities. Like Elijah Muhammad of the Nation of Islam after him, he preached and invited them to a brand of Islam that is well known for its heterodoxy. As this research will attempt to show, the MSTA which first manifested in Newark, NJ in the early 1900's was not a pacifist movement created in a vacuum as previously assumed by such esteemed scholars as E.U. Essien Udom, C. Eric Lincoln, Claude Clegg, Richard Brent Turner and others, but rather, its founder considered it to be an extension of the Moroccan Barbary state that had assisted the United States in its early

1

stages of political development. The details of this relationship reveal that there was a mutual understanding between the United States and Morocco concerning how each would conduct business with the other in matters of seafaring and commerce. This relationship made it possible for the subjects of both countries to enjoy the protection and benevolence of their respective governments. It was agreed that no Moor would be enslaved in the New World, and no American citizen could be enslaved in Moroccan controlled territories. We find evidence of this in the public records of U.S.-Moroccan relations. The U.S. Government sent its first official communication to the Sultan of Morocco in December 1780. It read:

> We the Congress of the 13 United States of North America, have been informed of your Majesty's favorable regard to the interests of the people we represent, which has been communicated by Monsieur Etienne d'Audibert Caille of Sale, Consul of Foreign nations unrepresented in your Majesty's states. We assure you of our earnest desire to cultivate a sincere and firm peace and friendship with your Majesty and to make it lasting to all posterity. Should any of the subjects of our states come within the ports of your Majesty's territories, we flatter ourselves they will receive the benefit of your protection and benevolence. You may assure yourself of every protection and assistance to your subjects from the people of these states whenever and wherever they may have it in their power. We pray your Majesty may enjoy long life and uninterrupted prosperity.[3]

Further, we learn from the pioneering efforts of Amir Muhammad, Director of Collections and Stories of American Muslims (CSAM), a Washington D.C. based research institution, that "in 1787 on the Delaware River, a Treaty of Peace and Friendship was signed between the United States and Morocco bearing the signatures of Abdel-Khak, Muhammad Ibn Abdullah, and George Washington."[4]

18TH CENTURY MOORS TEST U.S.-MOROCCAN TREATY

At the beginning of the next decade, the treaty was tested. Around 1790, at a time when the American slave system was at its height, the Sultan of Morocco petitioned the United States government to give special accommodations to those classified in America as Moors. "Free Moors by the names of Francis, Daniel, Hammond, and Samuel, along with their wives Fatima, Flora, Sarah and Clarinda asked the South Carolina House of Representatives to treat them as free whites.' "They petitioned the legislature to rule that they were not subject to the laws that governed other blacks and slaves."[5] This petition resulted in the passage of the Moors Sundry Act, which was enacted by the legislative body of South Carolina to grant special status to the subjects of the Sultan of Morocco. The Free Moors were quick to remind their American hosts of the earlier covenant and, based on the sanctity of that covenant, resisted all attempts by the Americans to violate it.

This action by the Free Moors and the Sultan cannot be fully understood without taking into account the long-standing differences between Islam as a civilization, and Western culture as a civilization separate and distinct from Islam and all others that preceded it. Unlike Western civilization, Islamic civilization did not place emphasis on skin color or ethnocentrism, but rather religion. Further, the separation of Church and State was not a characteristic of any African society of that day, whether it was dominated by Islam, a Traditional African Religion or a mixture of the two. Thus, set apart primarily by their desire to preserve their privileged political status in the American racial caste system, these Free Moors sought to voluntarily ostracize themselves from all others brought here from Africa, whether slave or free. The motivation behind this, however, was to obtain the highest level of freedom, as oppose to identifying with white society. Further, because of the diplomatic relations that the United States had with Morocco in the early part of its history others, from West Africa, who were enslaved in the United States during the antebellum period, were able to, and did, petition for their freedom. A case in point is the story of the "Prince among Slaves," Ibrahima Abdur Rahman, a West African Muslim enslaved in Mississippi. A Senegalese scholar, Dr. Sylviane Diouf states:

> The road to freedom had opened up for Ibrahima Abdur-Rahman a few years earlier when, enslaved in Mississippi, he had decided to send a letter to his family. On October 3, 1826, his friend Andrew Marschalk sent his letter, written in Arabic, along with a cover letter to Thomas B.Reed, a United States senator from Mississippi. In his own letter, Marschalk noted that Ibrahima's epistle, as stated by the writer, was to inquire about his family, hoping to join them. Marschalk also mentioned that Ibrahima claimed to belong to the the royal family of Morocco. This, obviously, was not the truth. Andrew Marschalk may have purposely invented that story; by claiming that Ibrahima was related to the reigning family of Morocco, he was almost certain to attract attention and fast action on behalf of his friend. Whereas the United States had diplomatic relations with Morocco, it had none with Futa Jallon, Ibrahima's own region.[6]

"When the Moroccan authorities had learned of Abdur Rahman's situation they took the matter very seriously; they told the U.S. consul that they were eager to have their coreligionist freed and would pay for the expenses."[7] The end result was that Abdur-Rahman was freed. In addition to Abdur Rahman's literacy in helping to pave his way to freedom (as noted by Diouf), one could argue persuasively that Morocco's diplomatic ties to the U.S. was another major factor that contributed to his becoming free. Therefore, during the time of the American Revolution, Morocco became the protector of Muslims and the defender of Al-Islam in the western hemisphere in several significant ways. Morocco reinforced in many Muslims enslaved in the Americas a national consciousness that recognized Islam as the dominating cultural, social and religious influence in their lives. This asserted diplomacy by the Moroccans made it possible for many American Muslim slaves to evade the American slave system. It also reinforced in the minds of many African Muslim slaves the idea that Morocco best represented their desire for independence from the American slave system and the right to identify with the religion and culture of Islam.

NOBLE DREW ALI LINKS HIS
MOORISH COMMUNITY TO MOROCCO

These developments would only become significant again in the early twentieth century with the rise of the Moorish Science Temple of America. Noble Drew Ali, from his base in Newark, NJ taught his followers that they were the descendants of Moroccan citizens who at one point in history were protected by the treaty that had been established between the United States and the Moroccan government. Their connection to Morocco protected them from becoming slaves in America. In response to the question, why is it important to know about your forefathers, Newark resident Mendheim Bey, a practicing Moorish American since the early 1930's stated, "so nobody will be able to make a slave out of you; you can get your equal rights." For those who are familiar with Moorish American teachings, Bey's reply registers as a classic Moorish American response. In his view, as in that of so many others, nationality was the element that served as one's major source of security in the global mix. Drew Ali understood that it was your nationality that identified you as a citizen of the world. Indeed, most average young Moorish Americans are very well versed in early American-Moroccan relations. Consequently, their present identity and struggle is closely tied to the issues and problems that Africans in America faced during that era. Although these Moroccans were small in number compared to those that had been shipped here from West Africa from the early 1600s through the infamous Middle Passage, they clearly had a greater political impact on U.S. Congressional decisions in matters of citizenship, and they did not hesitate to take advantage of their privileged political status. Sadly, in the end their rights like those of all non-Europeans were eventually relegated to an inferior status as the American slave system in the newly formed United States of America became more institutionalized and intimately tied to what became the racist doctrine of the White Man's Burden. The struggle of the Free Moors like that of all Africans enslaved in the Americas then became a struggle against white racism and white rule.

COMMONALITIES BETWEEN
MOROCCO AND THE NEW REPUBLIC

With respect to why Morocco extended itself to America's founding forefathers in the first place, historian Sherrill B. Wells states,

> The Moroccan Sultan's overture was part of a new policy he was implementing as a result of his recognition of the need to establish peaceful relations with the Christian powers and his desire to establish trade as a basic source of revenue. Faced with serious economic and political difficulties, he was searching for a new method of governing which required changes in his economy. Instead of relying on a standard professional army to collect taxes and enforce his authority, he wanted to establish state-controlled maritime trade as a new, more reliable, and regular source of income which would free him from dependency on the services of the standing army. The opening of his ports to America and other states was part of that new policy.[8]

This early relationship between the adherents of Islam and the social and political engineers of the new republic was in part characterized by a common vision and yearning to advance the greater good of society while promoting a free enterprise economic system and individual rights. Few Americans are prepared to accept the fact that the principles of Islam were, and in many ways still are, consistent with the vision of America's founding forefathers in their dedication to human reason, science and education as the best means for building a stable society of free men and women on earth. The reality is that Morocco had much in common with America in spite of the fact that it was a Muslim country.

MUHAMMAD ALEXANDER RUSSELL WEBB:
AN AMERICAN VOICE FOR ISLAM

The African American contribution to the development of Islam in the United States must be understood and examined in its proper historical context. Dr. Akbar Muhammad of Binghamton University states, "it is widely believed that historically the first Muslims of American birth were the product of immigrant Arab proselytization among poor African Americans."[9] This myth has caused many Americans to view al-Islam as simply a "black man's religion" or an "Arab religion." Few Americans are aware, he states, that

> the first recorded American convert to Islam seems to have been a rather obscure European American, the Reverend Norman, a Methodist missionary in Turkey who embraced Islam in the 1870s," only five years after the Civil War . . . he was followed in the next decade by another European American, Muhammad Alexander Russell Webb. And, contrary to popular belief, "the earliest organization to attempt directly the conversion of Americans to Islam seems to have been the American Islamic Propagation movement. Founded in 1893, it was headed by the erudite and imposing Muhammad Webb . . . Either as publisher or editor, Webb was said to have worked for more than seven newspapers in various cities in Missouri, New York and New Jersey.[10]

These facts of history pose a serious challenge to those who believe that Islam in America in the early 20th century was restricted to the African American and immigrant Muslim experience. It is also important to mention that Webb's interest in al-Islam was not superficial or motivated by some ulterior motive, but, rather, he was one who out of conviction was deeply influenced by its simplicity and comprehensive approach to life. Further, Webb did not neglect to express this allegiance outwardly. He very often wore Eastern style dress, a long beard, and a white turban. "Webb believed that western clothing signified western decadence and could ultimately lead to the moral corruption of Muslims."[11] In 1892, this European American responded to a query about his conversion to Islam. He stated:

> I adopted this religion because I found, after protracted study, that it was the best and only system adapted to the spiritual needs of humanity. . . . About eleven years ago I became interested in the study of Oriental religions . . . I saw Mill and Locke, Kant, Hegel, Fichte, Huxley, and many other more or less learned writers discoursing with a great show of wisdom concerning protoplasm and monads, and yet not one of them could tell me what the soul was or what became of it after death . . . my adoption of Islam was not the result of misguided sentiment, blind credulity, or sudden emotional impulse, but it was born of earnest, honest, persistent, unprejudiced study and investigation and an intense desire to know the truth. The essence of the true faith of Islam is resignation to the will of God and its corner stone is prayer. It teaches universal benevolence, and requires purity of mind, purity of action, purity of speech and perfect physical cleanliness. It, beyond doubt, is the simplest and most elevating form of religion known to man.[12]

Webb's testimony illustrates that, although such men clearly represented an extremely small minority, orthodox or Sunni Islamic thought was not non-existent or altogether taboo among native-born Americans of European ancestry prior to the early 20th century. This is significant for two reasons. First, it refutes the idea that Islam is the exclusive birthright of blacks, as the followers of Noble Drew Ali and Elijah Muhammad were led to believe. Secondly, the harsh treatment that Webb received from other white Americans shows that there was something about Islam that did not sit right within certain elite circles. In fact, Webb preceded the emergence of Islam as a religious and nationalistic phenomenon amongst African Americans. As it seems, Webb was not as successful in gaining converts as his African American successors who, against great odds, established a foundation and a clear model for Muslim community development in many urban centers of the United States. Nevertheless, it is possible that Drew Ali was influenced indirectly by Webb. It is probable that Dr. Akbar Muhammad was informing his colleagues in the American academy of this possibility when he stated that "there can be little doubt that Webb and other members of his association influenced subsequent efforts to establish Islam in the United States."[13] On the other hand, both Webb and Drew Ali were said to have traveled to Muslim lands and consequently were tutored by foreign Muslims. Although they ministered to different audiences in the U.S, perhaps there is a link to be found in this broken chain of American Muslim community developers. Nevertheless, Dr. Akbar Muhammad informs us that "at least two memorial meetings have been organized in Webb's honor, the last being as late as 1943."[14] As is quite evident, Webb's audience was primarily comprised of white American intellectuals and the academic community. Drew Ali concentrated his efforts on directing African Americans towards the Muslim East.

ISLAM, AFRICAN-AMERICAN MUSLIMS AND THE WEST

In the early part of the 20th century, native born Americans who identified with the religion of Islam, though a growing influence, were considered insignificant, and seemingly were not taken very seriously by the government. One could reasonably argue that in addition to race, religion for these sons and daughters of the soil was a key impediment to upward mobility. It is likely that some government attitudes were shaped by international factors. From a national point of view, the Ottoman (Turkish Islamic) Empire, because of its association with the Axis powers during World War I, was declared by U.S. officials an enemy to freedom and democracy. The Axis Powers were eventually defeated and the slogan "make the world safe for democracy" was popularized. Since this defeat, the Western powers have worked hard to prevent such a threat from rising again anywhere in the world, especially on American soil. And since it was believed that the presence of Islam in a global context posed a serious challenge to Western ideals and culture, Muslims of African ancestry were stigmatized not only because of their black skin and African features, but also because of their Islamic heritage, which was viewed by most European Americans as inferior. All of these, in the minds of the white Anglo Saxon Protestant male, were considered un-American.

Although Protestant forms of religious expression had by this time dominated the American religious consciousness, thereby managing to check more orthodox Christian and Jewish influences, the encounter with Islam in the early 20th century was an entirely new challenge for the American social structure. This challenge was further complicated by the history of the relationship between Muslim immigrants and non-Muslim immigrants. Dr. Akbar Muhammad states, "the life of the Muslim immigrant was a difficult one relative to that of his or her Christian countryman who often was aided by American missionary organizations, churches, and individuals."[15] "Neither Islam nor the Ottoman (Turkish) Empire, which officially ruled much of the Arabic-speaking and Eastern European lands, had been endeared to the American heart."[16] To most Americans, Islam, particularly the way that it evolved within the African American experience, was viewed as a counter-culture that was out to destroy Western civilization. This perceived threat caused the American government and its various institutions to declare war on the cultural and religious practices of Americans who chose Islam as their way of life. Thus, as quiet as kept, these communities were oft-times used as scapegoats not only by whites, but by other African Americans who did not share their cultural and religious sentiments.

NOTES

1. Amir Muhammad, *Muslims in America: Seven Centuries of History (1312–2000)* 2nd Ed., (Beltsville, Maryland: Amana Publications), 18.

2. Allan Austin, *African Muslims in Antebellum America: Transatlantic Stories and Spiritual Struggles*, (New York: Routledge, 1997), 13.

3. http://www.usembassy-morocco.org.ma/US_Moroccan_Relations1.htm

4. Amir Muhammad, 18 and 19.

5. Amir Muhammad, 21.

6. Sylvianne Diouf, *Servants of Allah: African Muslims Enslaved in the Americas*, (New York: New York University Press, 1998), 137.

7. Diouf.

8. Sherrill B. Wells, "Long-Time Friends: A History of Early U.S.-Moroccan Relations 1777-1777-1787," http://www.usembassy-morocco.org.ma/US_Moroccan _Relations1.htm

9. Akbar Muhammad, "Muslims in the United States: An Overview of Organizations, Doctrines, and Problems," In *The Islamic Impact*, eds. Yvonne Yazbeck Haddad, Byron Haines, and Ellison Findly, (Syracuse, New York: Syracuse University Press, 1984), 197.

10. Akbar Muhammad, *Muslims in the U.S.*

11. Richard Brent Turner, *Islam in the African American Experience,* (Bloomington: Indiana University Press, 1997), 65.

12. Akbar Muhammad, "Overview of Organizations," 198.

13. Akbar Muhammad, "Overview of Organizations," 199.

14. Akbar Muhammad, "Overview of Organizations."

15. Akbar Muhammad, "Overview of Organizations," 197.

16. Akbar Muhammad, "Overview of Organizations."

Chapter Two

A City Ripe for Settlement

NEWARK AT THE TURN OF THE 20TH CENTURY

In the year 1912, only one year before the Islamic influence established a traceable presence in Newark, "the City of Opportunity," as Newark became known, had no place to go but up, states John T. Cunningham in his study entitled *Newark*. . . .Peter J. Leary, who provided an Illustrated History of Essex County for the Board of Trade in 1891 wrote that "Newarkers themselves have begun to awaken to a realization of what their city really is, and of its magnificent possibilities . . ."[1] People were beginning to realize that, with respect to the number of people who had skills and the practical know-how at the dawn of Newark's industrial age, Newark was a "sleeping—and often much abused giant. At the turn of the century, the people at this time, more than any other time since the Civil War, pooled together to improve the appearance of the city. Great buildings were being erected in the downtown area, signifying to many that Newark was approaching a "golden age."[2] Between 1900 and 1916 Newarkers had significantly improved on the infrastructure of the city,[3] and many people began to reap the benefits of their labor. Jobs were plentiful, and most people were caught up in the spirit of progress. The new Essex County Court House on Warren Street, the street where some say that Noble Drew Ali resided when he settled in Newark, was completed in 1907. "It replaced the brownstone Egyptian-style Court House that was at the corner of Market Street and Springfield Avenue."[4] "The older structure, because of its small size could no longer accommodate county business."[5]

This so-called "golden age" was further marked by the establishment of parks and publicly displayed statues commemorating white men such as Robert Treat, who also had a hotel named after him, and the widely-celebrated Thomas Edison. 'A statue of Seth Boyden was erected in Washington Park in his honor, and also Frederick T. Frelinghuysen was similarly honored in Military Park.' 'Also, the two greatest American heroes, Presidents Lincoln and Washington, were memorialized through sculpture."[6] The legacy of these men has been preserved in the city as represented in the art of those who speak for the dominant culture. During this period, states Cunningham, "people generally found life to be simple, and business proceeded in courtly dignity."[7]

Religious conflict and ethnic strife was not uncommon, but it seemed to have taken a back seat to the general mood of progress. No doubt, Christianity played a major role in transcending ethnic differences. "Newark at that time constituted a conglomeration of small self-contained ethnic communities.'[8] 'By 1911, the Italians, the Irish, the Germans, the Jews, and the Slavs predominated in areas of the city that made each ethnic community distinct.' Whites constituted the majority of residents at that time, and the churches that they established aided in uniting most Newarkers on a social as well as a religious basis. As it seems, there was a mutual respect or at least a fairly decent working relationship between Protestants and Catholics. The Protestants had several churches. Among those frequented by mostly white residents were the "Trinity, Old First, North Reformed, Peddie Memorial, the House of Prayer, and Second Presbyterian." "Catholics took pride in the huge new Cathedral near present day Barringer High School on Parker Street." 'Work on this structure had begun in 1899 and according to historian John Cunningham, by 1902 the granite walls of the Cathedral were fifty feet high.' "By 1910 the front wall and towers stood ninety-eight feet above the ground."[9]

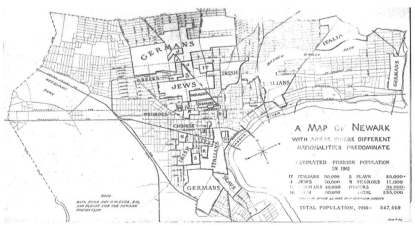

A 1911 map of Newark with areas where different nationalities predominate. Source: Social Service Charitable, Civic, Educational, Religious of Newark, New Jersey: A Classified and Descriptive Directory Compiled by A.W. MacDougall (Newark, NJ: Bureau of Associated Charities, 1912). (Courtesy of Newark Public Library.)

"Between 1910 and 1916 African Americans could be found in large and small patches all over the oldest part of the city, except in the Forest Hill, Roseville, Vailsburg, and Woodside sections."[10] For the most part their social and religious life was separate and distinct from that of white residents; African Americans generally formed their own congregations. "Between 1917 and 1932 the number of churches in Newark rose from 14 to 34 and by 1941 they numbered approximately 43.' 'Over one half of these churches were administered by the Afro-American Baptist State Convention, which accounted for the formation of fifteen black congregations in Newark between 1916 and 1941." [11] Indeed, as professor Clement A. Price observed, "the Negro Church provided the major social and cultural outlet for Afro-Americans prior to World War I."[12]

As a result of WWI things began to change rapidly. "The war brought thousands of new blacks from the Deep South into the city, most of them from areas whose characteristics were vastly different from Newark's social, political and religious life."[13] American commercial and political leaders capitalized on the opportunity for cheap black labor as they prepared for the war against the Germans, the Hungarians and the deteriorating Ottoman Empire. Because this was primarily a European war, European immigration into the United States had virtually ceased. Price states that, "New Jersey's industrial interests actively encouraged the migration of African Americans from the south to northern cities such as Newark.' 'Munition plants, brick yards, wire factories, and other war related firms—many for the first time—considered African Americans as a source of labor."[14] It is against this background that some African Americans that migrated to the city of Newark began their efforts of Muslim community development.

THE GREAT MIGRATION'S IMPACT ON NEWARK

It is essential to understand that "before WWI African Americans were a small and dispersed minority in the city's population and that at that time there were few instances of overt hostility against them."[15] The war brought many southerners to Newark that were not familiar with the northern routine. They came by way of what historians describe as the Great Migration. This, quite naturally, brought new challenges to Newark officials and to the citizenry. Although the industrialists had gotten the necessary man-power to maximize profits, the social condition of the city had worsened. Inadequate housing and healthcare became important issues that took center stage as ambitious and aspiring public officials realized that the influx of people from the southern United States and from eastern and southern Europe would put a strain on the city's resources. As the record shows, of all immigrants to Newark, African Americans who were sons and daughters of the soil were the most adversely affected by the problems confronting the city. By "1920 the Third Ward, which contained the greatest concentration of African Americans, was notorious for its disease and death . . . 'The Third Ward ranked first with cases of epidemic meningitis, erysipelas, influenza, and tuberculosis; and it was second in instances of typhoid fever, gonorrhea, and syphilis."[16] These problems put a strain on the upward mobility of the African American community.

It seems as though African-American migrants already influenced by the Islamic religion prior to coming to Newark were a part of this great migration. Drew Ali, for example, was from North Carolina; he had already been exposed to Islam. As with all migrations not only did these southerners bring their bodies, but they brought their ideas. Dr. Sulayman Nyang of Howard University assessed these developments as important. They have been important because of the inevitable impact that people influenced by Islam have had on the process of social change not only in African America but in all of America due to the power of ideas. Nyang asserts that it was through the internalization of religious ideas and cultural symbols borrowed from the Muslim World, and more importantly the simple *tauhidic* statement of *la illaha il-lallah, Muhamadur Rasulullah* (There is no God but Allah and Muhammad is the Messenger of Allah) that the Muslim African American contribution to the process of social change in urban America should be recorded in the memory of United States history.[17] Further, he asserts, since Islam undoubtedly is here to stay, social change perhaps will continue to be affected as more and more people internalize a *tauhidic* consciousness.[18] Although some of the contributors to this were of foreign stock that can be traced to the early period of American exploration by West Africans in the eighth century and later years, history teaches that the native born African American people, many of whom were the descendants of Africans brought to the Western hemisphere to be slaves in the 17th and 18th centuries, played an important role in the establishment of Muslim community life in the United States. Allan Austin's statement that "scholars have only recently begun to investigate possible connections between these early Muslims and Muslim movements that rose in the 1920s in the American North"[19] is quite interesting in this regard.

WHY ISLAM?

Many have asked why African Americans have been so attracted to Islam. While Austin's statement in the preceding chapter raises our eyebrows, there is no easy answer to this question. Nevertheless, it is true that in a broad sense, religion has been central to the African American ethos. History teaches that even before Africa's encounter with the three major branches of the Abrahamic tradition, namely, Judaism, Christianity and Islam, Africans were a deeply religious people who believed in God and had a concept of life after death.[20] Some scholars have argued that Abraham's religion, that is, the belief in the one, unseen and omnipotent God and the place of revelation in man's mental and spiritual consciousness, has left an indelible mark on all humans. For them, internalizing the *Tauhidic* idea is the most authentic expression of a human's willingness to return to his roots, rather than what African Americans have learned from studying the works of the Afrocentric scholars who believe and propagate the idea that ancient African (Egyptian) history and culture is and should be at the center of man's consciousness. This cold war certainly exists and must be examined more thoroughly by scholars in the new millennium. Nevertheless, the question of why so many African Americans are choosing Islam has made headlines in the world of journalism in the 1990s, and consequently is increasingly drawing the attention of pundits in the post 9/11 world. Although this hypothesis needs to be tested further, the consensus among Muslim American leaders is that Islam, and what it has to offer for shaping and re-shaping its adherents, has been successful in filling a spiritual void in the individual and collective lives of African Americans. Nevertheless, regardless of why many African-Americans have been attracted to Islam, a better question one might ask is: how has this phenomenon impacted America? This is a question that Americans need to seriously consider since Islam has proven to be the fastest growing religion not only in the African-American community, but in these United States and the world. The growth of Islam in Greater Newark alone has certainly impacted the lives of a number of people. As many African-Americans have internalized the idea of strict monotheism (*Tauhid*) they effected change in the neighborhoods where they settled. One of the main reasons why this became possible is due to the centrality of the mosque to Muslim community life. "The urban mosque in America, historically, has had an extended influence on the local communities in which they are situated in terms of economic growth and [especially] social life."[21] Newark Muslims have been involved in nurturing this process certainly since 1941 when Ezaldeen institutionalized the five pillars of Islam at his storefront mosque as a part of Newark's evolving urban culture. People then and now are called together five times a day to remember their Creator first, and then to socialize and network in the interest of the community. Thus, "the mosque is more than just a congregational space for worship; it has played an [important] social role as well."[22] Because people as a result of this Islamic influence are obliged to frequently come together, human interaction and development is always encouraged. Professor Nyang stated that "it will be evident that the three things that humans must synchronize in order for this process to take place indeed are--namely thoughts, words, and deeds."[23] Further, the right to freedom of conscience theoretically is a virtue that has existed in American society since its founding; and since this principle is not alien to Islam's own religious tradition, world view, or historical experience, Muslim Americans have had little difficulty exercising this right. Rather than seeing the right to freedom of conscience as a privilege of being a citizen of the United States, Muslim Americans have seen it, just as other Americans have, as a natural right given to humans by God. This means essentially, that the boundaries for exercising one's freedom of conscience should and must be defined by God. Some of America's earliest thinkers understood this, but the problem is that they were all products of the Western materialist philosophy that was influenced by the so-called Age of Enlightenment, which had no explanation on how to handle the living reality of man's soul. Therefore great minds such as George Washington, Thomas Jefferson and James Madison were able to defend the integrity of such enlightened documents that spoke for the people, but were not equipped to handle those who would exclude Native Americans, Africans and women from the commonwealth. As history teaches, Native Americans and Africans remained subjugated peoples and chattel slaves (property) after the War for American Independence was won and women were still without a political voice. Although there was a variance in methodology, the local lingo in Newark articulated by many of the spiritual leaders of this diverse community share a common belief that Islam is a comprehensive belief system that addresses the economic, political and spiritual needs of man, not only in his individual life but also in his collective life. They have understood that Islam from its inception declared itself in clear and unambiguous terms a universal religion for all.

African Americans have tried to make the best out of the difficulties of their lives. In a general sense, the greatest difficulty that minority groups experience is oft-times overlooked or misunderstood by others. Historically, for many African Americans who have chosen the Sunni Islam path, the greatest challenges have been reinventing themselves, and their mission in life in accordance with the concept of *Tauhid*, the foundation upon which the Islamic faith is built. The general feeling is that it has sometimes been a difficult path to tread in these United States, notwithstanding the fact that African American Muslims have tried very hard to be loyal to the principle in both theory and practice. The foundation of this difficulty began during the days of slavery. Kahera reminds us that "the American Muslim slave community, although very devout, was hindered by the subjugation and in-human treatment of slavery and by the restrictions placed on religious prac-tice in general among slaves."[24] Though clearly a heterodox group, the his-tory of the Moorish American community provides some examples of the African American attempt to recapture the spirit of *Tauhid*. In Newark's his-tory the earliest and clearest examples can be found in the Addeynu Allahe and the Baitul Quraish experiences. Although the Islamic faith which they all claimed to be apart of rests on the concept of *Tauhid*, it should be men-tioned that African Americans though committed to Islam have only re-cently begun to thoroughly examine and understand the depth of the simple, yet comprehensive declaration of the words *la illaha illallah, Muhammadur Rasullah* (there is no god but God and Muhammad is his Messenger.)

NOTES

1. John T. Cunningham, *Newark*, (New Jersey: New Jersey Historical Society, 1968), 222.
2. Cunningham, 232.
3. Cunningham.
4. Cunningham, 239.
5. Cunningham.
6. Cunningham, 242.
7. Cunningham, 242.
8. Cunningham, 232.
9. Cunningham, 244.
10. Cunningham, 244 and 245.
11. Clement A. Price "The Afro-American Community of Newark, *1917–1947*" Ph.D. diss., Ann Arbor Michigan, 1975), 14 n, 3.
12. Price, *Afro-American Community*, 81.
13. Price, *Afro-American Community*, 17.
14. Price, *Afro-American Community*, 13.
15. Price, *Afro-American Community*, 26.
16. Price, *Afro-American Community*, 13.
17. Clement Price, "The Beleaguered City as Promised Land: Blacks in Newark, 1917-1947, *A New Jersey Anthology*, 445.
18. Thoughts shared in his lecture given on the subject of "Islam and the African-American Contribution to Social Change," sponsored by the WARIS Cultural Re-search and Development Center in Irvington, NJ on August 22, 1998.
19. Nyang, Thoughts shared, "Islam and African-American Contribution."
20. Allan Austin, *African Muslims in Antebellum America: Transatlantic Stories and Spiritual Struggles*, (New York: Routledge, 1997), 10.

21. For an insightful discussion of African traditional religious thought and two branches of the Abrahamic religious tradition read Dr. Sulayman S. Nyang's, *Islam, Christianity and African Identity*, Amana Books, 1984.

22. Akel Ismail Kahera, *Deconstructing the American Mosque: Space, Gender and Aesthetics*, (Austin, Texas: University of Texas Press, 2002), 93.

23. Nyang, Thoughts Shared, "Islam and the African American Contribution."

24. Kahera, 147.

Chapter Three

A Seed is Planted

THE MOORISH-AMERICANS: A GLIMPSE
INTO THEIR HISTORICAL SIGNIFICANCE

The Islamic influence in Newark began in 1913 with Noble Drew Ali. Born Timothy Drew, Noble Drew Ali was the first in the Greater Newark, New Jersey area who publicly declared belief in Islam. He migrated to Newark from North Carolina during the time of the "Great Migration"—when 1.5 million African Americans uprooted themselves from the southern states and came up North in search of jobs and a better life. Although his teachings were inconsistent with many of the orthodox Islamic views and practices which predominate in Newark today, it was under his leadership that the term Islam was first popularized by any organized group in the state of New Jersey. He founded a social and religious sanctuary in Newark in 1913, which he named the Caananite Temple, somewhere in the vicinity of Rutgers and Bank streets,[1] as a response to the discrimination and racism experienced by African American residents. Noble Drew Ali himself was said to have lived on Warren Street, according to a Moorish American Newarker named Mendheim Bey who said that his father met Drew Ali in the early part of the 20th century when he was first introduced to his teachings. Drew Ali claimed that the biblical Canaan was the land from which the inhabitants of present day Africa descended. The Bible classifies the Canaanites as a Hamitic people, an explicitly black people. (More will be said about the term Hamitic when the discussion moves to Muhammad Ezaldeen and the Addeynu Allahe Universal Arabic Association). Noble Drew Ali taught his followers about their alleged Moorish heritage, that their ancestors were Moors, and thus that they should be proud to call themselves Moorish Americans. As the late C. Eric

18

Lincoln stated in a chapter of his widely circulated study, *The Black Muslims in America*, "Drew Ali believed and taught that he was a prophet ordained by Allah, and that it was important for black people (Moors) to claim their nationality before they claimed a God.[2] This idea went against the grain of conventional Islamic orthodoxy, which had no such prerequisite for identifying with God, and clearly stipulated that Muhammad ibn Abdullah was a universal Prophet and God's last. Nevertheless, it was a religious expression that was internalized by a small group of African Americans at that time, which influenced subsequent groups. It should be known that although the numbers of the Moorish American community have declined significantly in Newark, small pockets can still be found by a thorough researcher.

The first Temple in Newark bearing the name Moorish Science was on the corner of Morton and Prince Street.[3] After a relatively short period of time the membership grew and it became necessary to expand. The organization was then successful in securing space in a larger building owned by Jews located at 230 Court Street.[4] This building was said to have had a capacity of about one thousand people. At these Moorish-American centers, the followers of Noble Drew Ali used to learn about the society of the ancient Moabites (present day Morocco), Moorish culture, and Islamic ethics and morality. A selected passage from their sacred book, *The Holy Koran of the Moorish Science Temple of America*, not to be confused with the Qur'an of orthodox Muslims, states:

Chapter XLV
The fallen sons and daughters of the Asiatic Nation of North America need to learn to love instead of hate; and to know of their higher self and lower self. This is the uniting of the Holy Koran of Mecca, for teaching and instructing all Moorish Americans, etc . . . The key to civilization was and is in the hands of the Asiatic nations. The Moorish, who were the ancient Moabites, and the founders of the Holy City of Mecca.[5]

Chapter XLVII
The Moabites from the land of Moab who received permission from the Pharaohs of Egypt to settle and inhabit North-West Africa; they were the founders and are the true possessors of the present Moroccan Empire.[6]

The above passages serve as a starting point for the reader to understand the origin of MSTA beliefs relative to an ancient identity. The following passage provides insight into the MSTA's idealism relative to the attainment of a perfect world society. Also in the sacred text, Noble Drew Ali stated:

Chapter XLVI
All nations of the earth in these modern days are seeking peace, but there is but one true and divine way that peace may be obtained in these days and it is

through Love, Truth, Peace, Freedom and Justice being taught universally to all nations, in all lands.[7]

Dr. Eric Lincoln was correct to conclude that "the Moorish Americans offered themselves as the nucleus around which a world of truth, peace, freedom, and justice must be built."[8] Despite their mistrust of and disdain for European Americans, "they stressed obedience and loyalty to the flag of the United States as long as they were to live in America."[9] Interestingly enough, the above passage seems to suggest that there was a strand of optimism in Noble Drew Ali's philosophy which did not exist in the later philosophies of Nation of Islam figureheads, Fard Muhammad or Elijah. Elijah Muhammad and his mentor, Fard Muhammad, took their radicalism to a higher level. They concluded that white America was eternally doomed because of the crimes it had committed against black humanity. White people, collectively, were depicted in the mythology of the Lost Found Nation of Islam as a race of devils. No such idea existed in Moorish American teachings. The devil, according to Moorish American teachings, was defined as the lower self. Further, this lower self had to be controlled, or better yet mastered by the higher self which was defined as the mother of the virtues and the harmonies of life, that breed justice, mercy, love and right.

By the 1930s the Moorish Americans became very popular in the major urban centers of northern New Jersey. Between New Jersey, especially in Newark and Jersey City, and Pennsylvania, there were as many as four thousand registered members of the MSTA. The attraction of African-Americans to the MSTA was partly in response to the deteriorating social and economic conditions faced by blacks in the city. There were also small pockets of Moorish Americans residing in places like Montclair, New Jersey. Mendheim Bey remembered a parade on Broad Street, Newark, which the Moorish American community participated in. The exact year is not known, but surprisingly, there was a time, he recalls, when Moors were able to wear their red *fezzes* without being harassed, all around in the streets. Eventually, Drew Ali, as chief spokesman of the Moorish American community, managed to establish a following in several other states which eventually culminated in a national organization. Not much is known with certainty about his experiences in Newark because records during the early stage of the organization's development were not preserved or made available to the general public. According to the research of Dr. Aminah Beverly McCloud, "there was a rather obscure man by the name of Dr. Suliman who assisted him with the Newark project."[10] However, we do know that Drew Ali left the city prematurely due to internal organizational problems. Some of the early pioneers in the Newark area who were familiar with this history had reason to believe that there were some doctrinal disagreements within the ranks which caused a split.

It is rumored that Fard Muhammad and his protege Elijah Muhammad the key figures of the Nation of Islam, also came through Newark sometime in the 1920s. Further, it is believed by some that the mysterious Fard may have provoked a split by introducing Drew Ali's followers to a new teaching. The evidence, however, is not conclusive. A publication of the Ansaru Allah Community, formerly a Brooklyn based organization states that "Noble Drew Ali's accomplishments in Newark were temporarily staggered by an Arab man named Abdul Wali Farrad Muhammad, who was said to have been from the Muslim Eastern country of Arabia."[11] Allegedly, this man came to Newark around the early 1920s and began teaching the Arabic language to a small group of black Americans who became interested in his version of Black Muslim thought. As one version of the story goes, many of Drew Ali's followers, who had already been orientated to his version of Islam since 1913, were impressed with this man, and as a result began to follow him. According to some reports, due to the internal animosities, which developed as a result of the arrival of this stranger, Drew Ali and a few of his dedicated supporters left Newark as early as 1916 and went to Pittsburgh, Pennsylvania to establish another community in that area. However, according to an official of the Moorish Science Temple based in Newark, NJ. and other MSTA members, Drew Ali's stay in Newark was much longer. As for the alleged stranger, his identity is not certain. Secondly, there is not sufficient documentation to comment on the exact nature or extent of his visit to Newark. It is highly probable that like most people who migrated to Newark at that time, he was attracted to its array of economic opportunities. Newark at that time was an industrial town, and jobs were plentiful. Yet, it is likely that the stranger's visit was relatively short since there is no record or indication that this man had any lasting influence among African Americans in Newark. Although he was not in Newark for a very long time, the possibility is great that he developed some form of relationship with members of the Moorish American community prior to 1930, but the evidence is not clear as to exactly when and where this connection occurred. Interestingly enough, one source states, "W. D. Fard, Elijah Muhammad's mentor, and founder of the organization known as the Lost Found Nation of Islam in 1930 was initially a leader of one faction in the Moorish Temple."[12] This idea is not a far-fetched one, particularly since we know that, by the time that Fard Muhammad came on the scene in 1930, the Moorish Science Temple of America organization had a national structure. "By 1928, Drew Ali was successful in setting up the Moorish Divine and National Movement of North America, Inc., which

served as an umbrella organization for fifteen temples."[13] In his widely circulated pamphlet, entitled "Islamic Roots In America," Imam Warith Deen
Muhammad acknowledged Drew Ali's contribution to the development of Islam in America, he states:

> Islam first became of interest to African Americans through a man called Noble
> Drew Ali who introduced his idea of Islam and it was preached from centers he
> called after the Moors as Moorish Science Temples. Most sources date the be-
> ginning of this influence at around 1913. It wasn't long after him, around 1930,
> that another man, a foreigner (Noble Drew Ali was not a foreigner) by the name
> of Fard who introduced a very extreme idea of Islam to the African American
> community. The organization now known as the Nation of Islam, and the
> founder of that idea, Fard, I believe studied the need in our community for a re-
> covery from slavery and then followed or imitated Drew Ali who set up the
> Moorish Science Temple. [14]

Organizational problems caused Noble Drew Ali to eventually leave the
city of Newark, and the Canaanite Temple which he started, to pursue his en-
deavors elsewhere. He was said to have started a community in Pittsburgh,
Pennsylvania before moving on to Chicago, Illinois where he established his
national headquarters.

Another group remained in Newark, and changed the name of the Canaanite Temple to the Holy Moabite Temple of the World ("Moabite" being a reference to the ancient name for Moroccans). By 1925, Drew Ali's influence
had reached Chicago, where the first temple bearing the name Moorish Holy
Temple of Science was founded. It was not until 1928 that the name was
changed to what it is known as today, the Moorish Science Temple of America (MSTA). By this time, nationally, the movement was composed of many
people, predominantly African Americans. "By 1928, Drew Ali's empire consisted of established temples in Charleston, West Virginia; Milwaukee, Wis-
consin; Lansing and Detroit Michigan, Philadelphia and Pittsburgh Pennsylvania; Pine Buff, Arkansas, Newark, New Jersey, Cleveland and Youngstown,
Ohio; Richmond and Petersburg, Virginia; and Baltimore Maryland."[15]

The creation of the MSTA was undoubtedly a response, in part, to the discrimination and racism experienced by African Americans. Even though New
Jersey was a northern state, race relations there were in some ways poor like
they were in southern states. Yet of all the northern states, the African American Islamic influence became most prominent there. This was an interesting
development since New Jersey's history of race relations was not very invit-
ing to blacks or people influenced by the Islamic faith. Much has been written about racial conflict. Historians have documented that "New Jersey has
had the worst race relations of the northeastern states."[16] "It was the only

Moorish-American man and boy studying. Courtesy of The Newark Public Library

northern state that failed to ratify the 13th, 14th, and 15th Amendments to the Constitution, and was the last northern state to enact legislation abolishing slavery . . .' 'With the possible exception of New York, New Jersey had the most severe slave code of the northern colonies . . .' 'Throughout the country's history, in its treatment of African Americans, New Jersey has often been likened to the South . . .' 'In 1823, for example, a traveler from Connecticut passing through New Jersey expressed a common northern view and called New Jersey "the land of slavery."[17] This social climate not only discouraged cooperation between the races, but also played a major role in fostering the *asabiya* (group solidarity) among the early Muslim pioneers that McCloud speaks of in *African-American Islam*. Giles Wright speaks of the conditions in NJ relative to black empowerment as a sort of paradox that has offered contrasting images.[18] "Viewed through the prism of the Afro-American experience, he states, NJ has been a place of hostility and hardship necessitating struggle, and yet a place of succor and opportunity permitting achievement."[19] The Moorish-Americans apparently were determined to take advantage of the opportunities available to them rather than be discouraged by the hostility of Christian whites and the hardship they would face in negotiating a space for their community. This was the climate in this state in which the seed to Muslim community development was born, and it was this climate that Islam first began to emerge as a nationalistic phenomenon among African Americans.

As previously mentioned, the Moorish-American influence was Newark's first public record of a community of people professing belief in the religion of Islam. At every level of its development, the African American community, as expressed through the philosophy of the MSTA, attempted to provide an alternative vision and lifestyle to the black masses. In this sense, it was very much like Marcus Garvey's Universal Negro Improvement Association (UNIA), though not as effective in mobilizing the black masses. The philosophy changed over time as African Americans who were influenced by Islam re-invented ways to define themselves and their condition in America.

Also significant is the connection between Drew Ali and Marcus Garvey. When Garvey came to the United States from his native Jamaica, he had aspirations to meet Booker T. Washington and use some of his teachings to help organize the black masses throughout the world, but Washington died before Garvey had a chance to meet him. Though there is little available evidence to support the contention that the activism of Drew Ali and Garvey was part of a grand plan, it seems safe to say that there was at least an implicit cooperation or tacit agreement between them. Although Garvey had not had the opportunity to developed relationships with Muslims in Jamaica until he went to England, Dr. Toni Martin's study, *Race First*, shows that in the early part of the 20th century Garvey was influenced by Islam through Duse Mohammed Ali, a prominent member of London's Islamic community. "Although Duse Ali resided in London, and was an Egyptian national of Sudanese-Egyptian parentage, he exercised a strong influence on the black nationalist movements within the United States."[20] "The *African Times and Orient Review*, a paper with international circulation published by Duse Ali was an anti-colonialist / anti-imperialist journal, which reported on significant persons, movements and events throughout the Third World."[21] Early in Garvey's career he worked for Duse at the newspaper office. Drew Ali apparently appreciated Garvey's commitment to the anti-colonial cause. It is appropriate to mention the Garvey / Drew Ali / Duse Ali connection here because of the tremendous influence that Garvey had in New Jersey, which became an important state for the growth of Garveyism. By 1926, there were 31 chapters of the UNIA in the state! This was at a time when the Moorish American influence was gaining momentum in the state as well. Further, the relationship between Garvey and Drew Ali is significant to this study because it shows that the early relationship between Islam and black-nationalism was rooted in an international Pan-African movement.[22] Martin has also documented the influence that the Ahmadiyyah Islamic Movement had on Gar-

vey's UNIA.[23] According to Martin, "Mufti Muhammad Sadiq, the leader of
this Muslim movement from India, was among the invited guests seated on
the rostrum at a New York UNIA meeting.' 'Sadiq's recent accomplishments
at that time were his conversion of some forty UNIA members to Islam."[24]
Garvey's ability to mobilize the black masses earned him the title the Black
Moses. But few have acknowledged the contribution of Islam and Muslim
support to Garvey's extraordinary success in establishing over 900 chapters
of his UNIA in 38 states and 42 countries by 1926.[25]

Interestingly enough, Noble Drew Ali referred to Garvey as the John the
Baptist of their movement. Their sacred text, the *Holy Koran of the Moorish
Science Temple of America*, states:

> In these modern days there came a forerunner, who was divinely prepared by the
> Great-Allah and his name is Marcus Garvey, who did teach and warn the nations
> of the earth to prepare to meet the coming Prophet; who was to bring the true
> and divine creed of Islam and his name is Noble Drew Ali . . .[26]

The essence of religion for Garvey was the imparting of race pride, Black
Nationalism and self-reliance. In this sense, he was very much like Elijah
Muhammad. The difference is that, unlike Elijah, he did not see a need to single out the white race as being a race of devils. Unlike the Nation of Islam
and the UNIA, the MSTA did not glorify blackness or put any emphasis on
the term which would suggest that African Americans should identify themselves as black people. To them black signified death. It was considered to be
a negative and meaningless way to define a people that were once a part of
the great Moorish Islamic empire which was comprised of a predominantly
dark skinned people. This also demonstrates the extent to which the Moorish
American community was influenced by orthodox Islam, which discourages
the classification of people by color. Also, this re-invention continued as
African Americans influenced by al-Islam in the Newark area became more
familiar with and dependent upon the primary sources of al-Islam namely, the
Qur'an and the Hadith literature.[27] As is evident, Drew Ali is a key figure of
Muslim history in New Jersey who obviously had some knowledge of al-Islam, but had little access or saw little need to promote its essential sources,
namely the Qur'an and the Hadiths, and thus did not emphasize the importance of them to his followers.[28] However, what Drew Ali had for his major
theological document was a book written by him composed of a conglomeration of teachings, concepts and ideas derived from Masonry, the Bible, and
the Qur'an. Yet, be that as it may, his MSTA organization was successful in
gaining recognition from city, state and federal officials as a fully incorporated Muslim or "Moslem," to use the term of that time, organization in the

U.S. They became known as Moors, and each member was required by Drew Ali to carry an identification card with the designation Moorish-American.

According to Hajj Heshaam Jaaber, a Sunni Muslim pioneer of the Greater Newark area, "when Noble Drew Ali issued one a membership card, he made it clear that this would connect him with the Qur'an of the holy city of Mecca."[29] In other words, it would point members toward founts of Islamic knowledge. This was the first attempt to encourage African Americans in Newark to turn towards the East, and to consider adopting the ways and traditions of the Muslim world. According to some, the purpose of his MSTA was not to proselytize or to give *dawah*,[30] as Muslims understand this term today, but to de-program its members from the long tradition of self hate that they had become accustomed to as a result of slavery, and to strengthen the political ties between them, Africa, and the rest of the Muslim world. His vision and goal was to re-educate the descendants of American slaves by teaching them about their heritage, which was said to be found in Morocco. This approach clearly neglected to shed any light on the marriage between the American and the rich West African cultural heritage that existed as a result of the interaction between West African Muslim slaves and southern slave owners. It is only recently that scholars such as Sylviane Diouf in her groundbreaking study, *Servants of Allah: African Muslims Enslaved in the Americas*,[31] have helped us to understand that Muslim West Africa, through the importation of African captives brought here to be slaves, has contributed much too American culture, art, rhythms and music. Two cases in point are the blues and jazz.

Every Moor was taught that he or she was a descendant of a great people from Morocco in North Africa who conquered Spain and much of Europe during the Medieval Period and gave it civilization. Drew Ali's program was largely religious, but it also had a political philosophy that did not espouse integration. As the evidence clearly indicates, his intent was to reorganize them in the Western Hemisphere as a productive, self-reliant and law abiding people as opposed to a lazy, dependant or rebellious people. Further, he wanted to use Islam influenced religion to help manage the economic and political affairs of this new micro-nation that he would build in the Western hemisphere under the auspices of the Moorish Science Temple of America. Perhaps the most important part of his teachings involved his efforts to teach his members about their religious rights under the U.S. Constitution. Drew Ali often spoke about the tensions that existed between the churches and the MSTA. In defense of his Moorish-American community he stated:

The Moorish Science Temple of America has received some opposition and criticism. The main opposition has come from certain Christian ministers. They have expressed themselves as being opposed to our propagation of the Mohammedan religion. Possibly because the promotion of the Mohammedan faith among our people in the United States is considered by them in terms as something new. Whatever the reasons may be for their opposition, the legal right to oppose citizens, individuals and organizations alike for their religious beliefs does not exist in the United States. The door of religious freedom made by the American Constitution swings open to all, and people may enter through it and worship as they desire. [32]

Followers of Noble Drew Ali have continued in Newark, where meetings traditionally have been held on Friday and Sunday at the Moorish Science Temples there. Compared to the 1930s, 40s and 50s, however, their numbers are small. National membership was published by September 7, 1934 *News* as over 100,000 and by September 16, 1949 the *Newark Star Ledger* as over 106,000.[33] The Moorish-Americans apparently sustained themselves in the city of Newark. At their gatherings, men would sit on the right side and women would sit on the left side of the Grand Sheik as he delivered a speech from the teachings of Noble Drew Ali. Unlike the juma'ah prayer services of the orthodox Islamic centers where believers sit on the musala (a special prayer rug designated for prayer rituals), believers at the MSTAs sat in chairs which were set up auditorium style like members of the church. Women usually wore white dresses and either red or blue turbans, while the men wore dark western style suits and the red Moroccan fez with a tassel hanging from the right side.

The religious services were structured in such a way where all members of the community shared in dispensing knowledge from the teachings of Noble Drew Ali. This was an obvious influence of the church on Moorish practices. After the Grand Sheik gave the keynote address, which usually involved some reference to the community's identification as Moorish Americans, and the need to cherish and preserve that identity, other members are invited to read passages from their sacred book and give praise and thanks to Almighty God, Allah, for sending them Noble Drew Ali as their prophet and guide. At these gatherings, members tended to remind one another of the simple things in life, such as the need to control one's negative thoughts, and the importance of being true to oneself. The congregation is reminded about the five principles of the universe, which are love, truth, freedom, peace and justice. The sum of these five principles was said to be Islam. McCloud states, "there is no clear evidence that Drew Ali had access to even the most basic of Islamic text, with the possible exception of the Qur'an."[34] Yet, his response to a member of his community to the question, what is Islam, was incredibly consistent with what orthodox Muslims believe. He stated:

Islam is a very simple faith. It requires man to recognize his duty toward God (Allah) his Creator, his fellow creatures. It teaches the supreme duty of living at peace with one's surroundings. . . . It is preeminently the religion of peace. The name means peace. The goal of man's life according to Islam is peace with everything. . . . The cardinal doctrine of Islam is unity of the Father (Allah). We believe in One God. Allah is all God, all mercy, and all power, He is perfect and holy, all wisdom, all knowledge, all truth. . . . He is free from all defects, holy, transcendent. He is personal to us in so far as we can see His attributes working for us but He is nevertheless impersonal, He is infinite, perfect and holy . . . nor do we believe that God is a helpless, inactive, inert force. Nothing happens without his knowledge and will. He neither begets nor is he begotten because these are traits of frail and weak humanity. This unity of Allah is the first and foremost pillar of Islam and every other belief hangs upon it.[35]

With respect to racial identity, the Moorish American community rejected the labels that European Americans tended to give to the African American community. Members were instructed not to use designations such as Black, Negro, or Colored, because these labels, in their reasoning, did not link them to any particular nation of the world. In their view, these labels were forced upon African Americans (Moors) by the Europeans to confuse them about their true identity, their God and their way of life. During the early days of the movement, all other Americans and immigrants could trace their roots to some particular country, but the same was not true in the case of people of African ancestry. Drew Ali stated the following with regard to this:

"If Italians, Greeks, English, Chinese, Japanese, Turks, and Arabians are forced to proclaim their free national name and religion before the constitutional government of the United States of America, it is no more than right that the law should be forced upon all other American citizens alike."[36]

For this reason, Morocco in North Africa was used as a sort of remote national symbol by the movement's founder, Drew Ali, to reconnect them to their roots. By the time that Drew Ali's influence had reached Chicago the various Moorish Science Temples of America, which had got their base from Newark, had established a political machine. "Rejecting the European-American designation, 'Negro,' as both derogatory and meaningless to blacks, members of Ali's community filled in "Moor" on federal, state, and city forms requiring the identification of ethnicity."[37] Mendheim Bey, a Moorish American of the Newark area says that to show the impact the organization had on the political system, members were able to get social security cards with their new Moorish name, a surname which consisted of El or Bey. It is likely that this occurred during Franklin D. Roosevelt's presidency. "The MSTA, although secretive, urged obedience to the American government and blended orthodox Islam with a respectability ethic."[38]

According to one estimate, "as many as thirty thousand African Americans have passed through the ranks of the organization prior to the Great Depression."[39] As is evident, "Ali and his followers offered blacks a new "Moorish" (or Moroccan) identity outside of the constraints of their status as Negroes and attempted to socialize them into a spiritual world in which a mythical "Asiatic" past was the central focus, states Claude Clegg.[40] The Islamic practices and influences were clearly evident. In addition to constructing a new nationality for blacks in response to white rejection, the Moorish Americans tried to rid African Americans of those vices, such as alcohol consumption and extramarital affairs, that they believed undermined the moral fabric of the African American community. Trends of Black Nationalism were already prevalent in many parts of urban America; thus, it was not surprising that the ideology of the Moorish Science Temple emerged when it did. However, what was surprising to many was the blend of Islamic and Black Nationalist fervor in the form of a special blend of African American Islam. Few are aware that "other prominent social reform leaders of the urban poor such as the men known as Daddy Grace and Father Divine were Moors before they branched out on their own."[41] These individuals left a legacy in Newark as well. Like Marcus Garvey's Universal Negro Improvement Association (UNIA), which had over 30 chapters in the state of New Jersey by 1930, the MSTA offered a contrasting ideology and style of protest to the integrationist movement as was represented by the DuBoisian school of thought. And although it is usually referred to as a cult or an insignificant entity in the writings of most researchers, careful examination of the influence of this organization will show that it was this seed that set the stage for the Sunni Muslim community that emerged in the 1940s and the Nation of Islam in the late 50s. In the late 1930s the Moorish American influence began to decline significantly, and another influence with a strong Sunni orientation, the Addeyu Allahe Universal Arabic Association, ushered in.

MOORISH-AMERICAN NOSTALGIA

In order to understand the nostalgia of the Moorish American community, it is useful to briefly comment on Noble Drew Ali's lineage and the history of the Moorish civilization which his organization claimed to be a part of. The Moorish American community thought of itself as being a part of the Islamic civilization that first began in Arabia and then extended into North Africa and eventually into Europe's Iberian Peninsula. One source states that "Drew Ali's father is said to have been a direct descendent of the Moors of Northwest Africa. His mother is believed to have been of Cherokee ancestry." This idea is not farfetched because, according to Dr. Virginia Easley DeMarce, a thorough researcher on African American and Native American relations, "there are thousands of African Americans from Virginia, and the Carolinas who claim Native American ancestry."[42] Interestingly enough, the *National Genealogical Society Quarterly* in the March 1992 issue featured an article by Dr. DeMarce, who while studying migration patterns took careful notice of an occurrence of those who were of mixed ancestry in the upper south.

With respect to his Islamic upbringing, it is said that "Drew Ali was taught in New York by a man named Djamel al Din al Afghani (1838–1897) who allegedly came to the United States in the winter of 1882–83.' 'Al Afghani is said to have been joined by his disciple and chief initiate, Muhammad Abduh.' 'The two missionaries supposedly had come to the United States to propagate the doctrine of ancestral and cultural pride under the banner of Pan Islam, which was meant to insure that the divine teachings of the ancestors were not forgotten among the Moors of North America."[43] Professor Ravanna Bey has stated that Drew Ali, beginning in his teenage years, had traveled extensively as a result of connections facilitated by al Afghani and Abduh. He would eventually, states Ravanna Bey, arrive in Egypt to experience Islamic culture. "While studying at Al-Azhar University, Drew Ali is reported to have come under the influence of Muhammad Rashid Rida (1865–1935 A.D.) and Aziz Ali al-Masri Bey (1878–1965 A.D.) as well as Marcus Garvey's mentor Duse Muhammad Ali-Effendi (1866–1945 A.D.) who lived in London, England at the time."[44] "Drew Ali is also said to have studied at the old Ethiopian College in Vatican City (Rome, Italy)."[45] When he eventually made available the "Moorish Science Koran" that he prepared for his members in 1926 there was an implied connection with the Sultan, Abdul Ibn Saud, who became the leader of Mecca in 1924. Saud was said to have been a descendant of Hagar, the mother of Abraham's first born, Ishmael. Hagar, a woman of black Egyptian stock, represents a symbolic link between Africa and Asia. These developments would have a profound influence on Drew Ali, the people who listened to him and the crystallization of a Moorish identity in America.

It is often said that the name Moor is related to the BlackaMoors, the African conquerors of Spain who were originally from Northwest Africa. The Muslims of the Iberian Peninsula (Spain and Portugal), who ruled Spain between 711 and 1492 C.E., are commonly known as the Moors. This great Moorish civilization, which blossomed in Spain in the early eighth century, was a highly developed Islamic civilization, and was ruled by dark-skinned peoples. At that point in history, these Muslims of Spain were more advanced technologically and educationally than all of Europe. Stanley Lane-Poole states in the introduction of his book, *The Moors in Spain*, "for nearly eight centuries, under the Mohammedan rule, Spain set all of Europe a shining example of a civilized and enlightened state.[46] Thus, it became essential for those who joined the Moorish-American community to learn about this important Islamic heritage. According to some researchers, the term "Moors" is a corrupted word referring to the people who came from Morocco, a Northwest African state. The Christians of the Iberian Peninsula began to use this term exclusively for Muslims when the Muslims lost administrative control of Northern parts of Spain and Portugal. The term Moorish then came to be synonymous with Islamic.

It is essential for students of Moorish American history to understand that being a Moorish American meant more than just being a part of a religious identity. It also meant that you were a part of a block that represented a political interest in the global arena. Noble Drew Ali wanted his Moorish American community to know that, historically, it was a part of that global reality. In addition to it being recognized as an ancient homeland, it was for this reason that he emphasized the importance of linking his Moorish-American community to the land of Morocco, and impressed upon all Moorish Americans the need to develop an international personality. Ali taught that the so-called "Negroes" were in fact Asiatics, and that all non-Caucasians were Asiatics; that all of the people in North America identified as "Negroes" were in fact Moors, descended from Moroccans who had immigrated here previous to the arrival of the European Caucasian.[47] According to Ali, they had had their Moorish citizenship and names taken away from them in 1779, and their Moorish names replaced by the slaveholder's names and referred to as "Negroes," "Colored" or "Blacks." To remedy this problem, Noble Drew Ali gave them a flag (red, with a green five pointed star in the center and identical to that of Morocco); he gave them a nationality (Moor); a book (*Holy Koran* of the MSTA); and an identification card which read in part:

> This is your Nationality and Identification card for the Moorish Science Temple of America. . . . We honor all the Divine Prophets, Jesus, Mohammed, Buddha, and Confucius . . . I do hereby declare you a Moslem under the Divine laws of the Holy Koran of Mecca, Love, Truth, Peace, Freedom and Justice. It ended with: I Am A Citizen of the U.S.A. [48]

It was also claimed that Drew Ali met with President Woodrow Wilson, who allegedly told him "it would be as difficult getting Negroes to accept Islam, as trying to get a horse to wear pants; you won't get a hundred of them."[49] As a form of protest, Drew Ali taught members of his community that they were to refer to themselves as a separate nationality. According to one Moorish American elder in Newark, Drew Ali's rationale was that in order to learn Islam, one had to know oneself. Further, it was reasoned that you

can't be Negro, Black and Colored and regain your rightful place in the
world, because Negro, Black and Colored didn't have a traceable history.
Thus, it was reasoned that in order to be truly free, you had to first get your
nationality. Drew Ali was not the first to protest the labels that Europeans
used to describe African-Americans or to claim an alternative identity for
those influenced by Islam.

As Alan Austin states, "there were some African Americans who maintained that they were not wholly or only African or black."[50] Several small
populations, Free Moors of the Carolinas (Drew Ali was from North Carolina) Mulungeons in Tennessee, Delaware Moors, and Virginia Maroons,
have insisted upon Muslim beginnings from colonial times.[51] This suggests
that these African Americans not only resisted European-imposed labels, but
were also not interested in severing the ties between them and their Islamic
faith. Also, implicit in this statement is the view that these people attempted
to trace their roots in this country to a class of African Americans that was
free and considered themselves linked in some way to the land of Morocco or
other parts of the world where Islam was prevalent. Indeed, many of the
Africans brought to the new world were fluent in Arabic and had extensive
knowledge in Islamic law which speaks to the extent to which Islam influenced their thoughts and lives. Commenting on the nostalgia of well known
African Muslim figures who became victimized by the American slave system, such as Job Ben Solomon, Ibrahim Abdur-Rahman, Bilali Mohammed,
Salih Bilali, Umar Ibn Said and others, Austin states:

> They were trained so well in the tenets of their faith that nearly all adhered to
> the religion of their parents despite years of blandishment by Christian mission-
> aries in the New World. Nearly all wished to return to Africa, despite witness-
> ing the wonders of the Western World and despite what must have been trau-
> matic experiences in the Old. The majority had impressive models back home
> and did not—as some latter day theorists have presumed—feel the need to adopt
> white role models.[52]

There is no clear evidence which would suggest that Drew Ali had any
specific knowledge of these African Muslims enslaved in America, nevertheless, he developed and instituted a program that was consistent with his
desire to preserve an Islamic heritage among people of African ancestry in
the West. Although the MSTA today is oft-times regarded as an insignificant
reality in the development of Muslim American social history, my research
shows that it played a major role in shaping not only a segment of America's
social and religious history, but that it also had a significant impact on the
development of political thought within the African American religious experience.

Few Sunni Muslim groups among African Americans in the area are prepared to accept the connection of Moorish American contributions to the development of Islam in the Western hemisphere. The Moorish American contribution is somewhat of a forgotten history, and in some circles regarded as
taboo. However, there are some groups, particularly those whose beginnings
began in the old Lost Found Nation of Islam and Ezaldeen's AAUAA, that
have outwardly expressed an appreciation of this African American contribution to the development of the Islamic faith in this part of the world. It is my
belief that this unfortunate reality is mostly due to the scarcity of information
and solid documentation concerning this group, and to some extent the influence that the practices and views of some immigrant Muslims (mainly Arab
and Pakistani) have had on African Americans since the late seventies. Their
brethren, due to their separate experience with the Deen, have introduced a
certain methodology with regard to propagation of the faith; one that pro-
poses that local and regional histories and experiences have little to do with
the development of a global Islamic consciousness. To their detriment, this
methodology has encouraged some well meaning African American Muslims
to ignore their own historical experience. Up until the late seventies, African
American Muslims were the major players in shaping the way that Islam was
understood and practiced in Newark. The leadership of Muhammad
Ezaldeen, Kamil Wadud and James 3X Shabazz lends considerable support to
this claim. With the securing of a massive structure in the downtown section
of Newark on Branford Place by Egyptian Muslims, the 80s, it seems, was in-
dicative of a growing immigrant influence on business life, though African
Americans still were the major players in establishing and maintaining the
business of the *masajid* on South Orange Avenue and Central Avenue in East
Orange, and a couple of Islamic schools. In the 1980s African Americans, primarily Muslim women, played a key role in developing and operating a full-
time Muslim school at the Islamic Cultural Center on Branford Place. It was
not until the 1990s that African American Muslims in the East Orange area
established two additional Islamic centers and an elementary school and high
school for the youth. Many of these men and women were oriented to Islam
through either the Nation of Islam or the Addeynu Allahe Universal Arabic
Association. Among them are those who do not see the relevancy of studying
about the Islamic influence in the American context, preferring only to seek
an understanding of Islam through the study of Arab history and culture, or as
some say, through the first generation of Muslims. Some have opted to take a
purely nonracial approach to understanding the history of Islam in the United
States. Their reasoning is that time is best spent on learning the Qur'an and
the Sunnah of the Prophet. And since understanding local histories is not a
prerequisite for this, many have wrongfully castigated this approach as a

bi'da (a religious innovation).[53] This is particularly tragic for African American Muslims because their history, so deeply entrenched in the color-conscious maladaptive world of American society, is so crucial to the development and growth of Islam, not only in Newark, but in the whole of the United States. Just as Islam had to transform a backwards Arab society that was once steeped in idolatry, sexism, and tribalism; where infant girls were buried alive by arrogant men who took great pride in fathering sons, so did it transform the thinking of African Americans who were victimized by a brutal form of slavery (chattel slavery), and institutionalized racism. The psychological effects of slavery and institutionalized racism were two American realities that were so pervasive that it dehumanized African Americans, and restricted their activities socially, economically, and politically. Thus it was white racism that produced a new cluster of African Americans whose response to it was not only to convey to the world the magnitude of what white over black actually meant, but also to offer an alternative to the ethnocentric approach to nation building promoted by the West. In other words, African American Muslims were, and still are, very interested in exercising their birthright to share their thoughts on how best to achieve an American society and a world that is based on freedom, justice and equality. They have always believed that there must be a revolution of the mind, and that that revolution should start in the culture of the American people. As Imam W.D. Mohammed stated at a Newark conference public address whose theme was "Support in Religion for Social Dignity and Community Empowerment," "true revolution brings about an evolution . . . and accordingly, the one who claims the title of revolutionist cannot claim success, unless that revolution evolves the people's intellect."[54] Once African American Muslims embraced the concept of Tauhid, the obsession with color and race subsided. The best example to illustrate this point can be found in the experience of the Nation of Islam after 1975. As one of the faithful stated, "Imam W.D. Muhammad had taken us to a whole new plateau." In the Newark chapter it was their internalization of the concept of Tauhid that tried to set things on equal footing between the black man and the white man. Likewise, it was the concept of Tauhid from its inception that implanted in the minds of all Muslims that all men and women were created equal in the sight of Allah. Further, the indigenous Sunni Muslim majority in the Newark area have done very little to document its history and make it available to the public.

Not much is known about Drew Ali's early experiences in Newark. However, an organization by the name of the Nubian Islaamic Hebrews: Ansaaru Allah Community, originally out of Brooklyn, NY, has published a book entitled *Who Was Noble Drew Ali?* Interestingly enough this organization, although once at the helm of controversy among Muslims in Newark, has published over ninety-one pamphlets and booklets on their understanding of Islam."[55] It was the only Muslim-oriented organization in the Greater Newark area, outside of the small pockets of Moorish American remnants left, that attempted to convey the meaning of Noble Drew Ali's life and work. To mention this organization is significant to the subject because of its visibility in the downtown area of Newark in the 80s and the early 90s. It used to attract many from among the youth of New York as well as Newark, New Jersey. In fact, during the 1980s, and part of the 1990s, it was common to find the Ansaars, as they were commonly known, selling the organization's literature, all of which was written by the organization's founder, Isa Muhammad (aka Dr. York), incense and oils, and recruiting young African Americans on the corners of Broad and Market Streets, and all up and down Halsey Street. They seemed to have had a special appeal to young African American male teenagers. The members of this organization had a great respect for Noble Drew Ali's work. They also admired and respected the work of men such as Marcus Garvey. In their orientation, the Ansaars resembled what many have described as a cult with a black-nationalist bent. This perception was reinforced in the minds of most Muslims of the Greater Newark area by the Jamaican born Dr. Abu Ameenah Bilal Phillips, in his pioneering study, *The Ansaar Cult*.[56] This book, endorsed by Abdullaah ibn Ridn Al-Bidaah of Daarul-Ifta Riyadh, Dr. Ahmad Muhammad Ahmad Jalli of Sudan and Dr. Maneh Al-Johani of the World Assemby of Muslim Youth charged the leader of the Ansaru Allah Community with heresy and cautioned Muslims from joining its ranks or supporting its economic enterprises. In their literature, it was common to find images of the Prophets and Angels depicted as dark-skinned with African features. It was not common to find an Ansaar recruiting heavily on Branford Place due to the strong Sunni Muslim presence there, although at times some of them would visit the Islamic Cultural Center to offer their *salats*. (Prescribed daily prayers) They were easily identifiable by their style of dress, which was usually, for males, a long white thob,[57] black boots and a turban wrapped around their heads. Although women members of the community, on occasion, would accompany some of the men on these expeditions, it was not a common practice.

Historians have made many references to Noble Drew Ali's involvement with the Masons. This has discouraged many Muslims from taking an objective look at the life and works of this important figure who helped shape the formation and character of Muslim community development in the Greater Newark community. "Seemingly, he embraced certain customs and symbols from the Masonic Order primarily because he was supposedly a Mason of high degree and a Shriner."[58] "The uniform he often wore, for example, the names El and Bey adopted by his followers, and the title Noble are Masonic in content.'[59] "While the MSTA came into existence in 1913, it was not formally chartered (licensed as a religious organization) until 1928.' 'With that in mind any scholar, states Prince Farad, who researches MSTA antecedents should examine Masonic connections."[60] This is particularly crucial to unveiling the mystery of the early history of the Moorish American community in Newark, New Jersey and its ideological stance. The serious student of history can begin by examining the root of African American Freemasonry, which is the Prince Hall Lodge, founded in 1775. "Prince Hall, the most famous black mason of his time, was a Revolutionary War Veteran and abolitionist who established the African Grand Lodge of North America . . .' 'Hall branched out on his own in 1775 when the local white Masonic Lodge in Boston rejected his application for membership because of his African ancestry . . .' 'Although he actively served in the War for Independence on the side of America, the white masons in America would not grant the African Lodge a full charter.' 'Hall then turned to British masons who approved his application in 1787, the same year that the U.S. Constitution classified a male slave as three fifths of a human being for the purpose of determining representation in Congress.' 'It was under this British charter that Hall in 1791 became Provincial Grand Master of North America and began authorizing black lodges in other cities, notably Philadelphia and Providence, Long Island."[61] It is evident that Noble Drew Ali, in some sense, was inspired by the work of Prince Hall and is highly probable that "Drew Ali's incorporation of Masonic customs and mannerisms in the early twentieth century were probably transferred from the Prince Hall Lodges to the Moorish Science Temple of America." Like Hall in the eighteenth century, Drew Ali too in the late nineteenth and early twentieth centuries had to contend with racial discrimination by whites. Both leaders in their day made sacrifices to ensure that young black children would get a proper education. "For example, in 1796, when he failed to convince Boston's City Council to provide a school for black students, Prince Hall had the children taught in his own home and that of his son."[62] The Moorish-Americans, following the advice of their self proclaimed prophet, Noble Drew Ali, would make similar sacrifices, except that they would incorporate Islamic teachings with masonry, black-nationalism and other eastern philosophies.

Although the Moorish Americans did not place much emphasis on the life of the Arabian Prophet, Muhammad Ibn Abdullah, they felt remotely connected to him, and attested to that through such things as diet, modest dress, fasting and rejection of the Trinitarian concept of God espoused by most Christians. They lived modest and simple lives, often giving salutations of peace to one another on a daily basis and facing towards the East during prayer. Instead of using the Muslim greeting—*As Salaamu Alaikum*—they would greet one another by raising the right hand with palm facing outward, saying either Peace or Islam. The Moorish-Americans provided the only Islamic influence in Newark up until 1941, the year that the next major Muslim organization among black Americans was founded, the Addeynu Allahe Universal Arabic Association (AAUAA). It was the AAUAA with its emphasis on a Black Hamitic Arab identity for its membership rather than a Moorish American one that became the first serious competition to Drew Ali's program and philosophy in Newark.

NOTES

1. Mendheim Bey, Interview by author, Newark, NJ, 17 August 1998.

2. C. Eric Lincoln, *The Black Muslims In America,* (New York: Kayode Publications, 1973), 56.

3. Bey, "Interview," 98.

4. Bey "interview." This building was demolished as a result of the urban renewal project under the auspices of the city of Newark.

5. Noble Drew Ali, *The Holy Koran of the Moorish Science Temple.*

6. Noble Drew Ali, *Holy Koran of MSTA.*

7. Noble Drew Ali, *Holy Koran of MSTA.*

8. C. Eric Lincoln, 57.

9. C. Eric Lincoln, 57.

10. Aminah Beverly McCloud, *African American Islam,* (New York: Routledge 1995), 10. This book is essential reading for those interested in the broad spectrum of Islamic expression within the African-American Muslim community. It looks at some of the diverse community histories, beliefs and practices that comprise African-American Islam.

11. Isa Sayyid, *Who was Noble Drew Ali?* (Brooklyn, NY.: Ansaru Allah Community, 1980) 8. This organization is now a defunct organization that has relocated out of state. Most Sunnis of the area regarded it as a heterodox group due to its nationalistic views, alleged sacrilegious practices, and anti-white views. For an in-depth discussion, see *The Ansar Cult* by Abu Ameenah Bilal Phillips. Riyadh Saudi Arabia:Tawheed Publications, 1988.

12. John H. Bracey, August Meir, & Rudwick Elliot, *Black Nationalism in America*, eds. (Indianapolis and New York:, Bobbs-Merrill Company Inc., 1970.), xlvi.

13. McCloud, *African American Islam*, 11.

14. W. Deen Mohammed, "Islamic Roots in America: An Interviewed with Imam W. Deen Mohammed and the British Broadcast Corporation (BBC) at *Muslim Journal*," July 1993 in Chicago, Ill.

15. McCloud, *African American Islam*, 11.

16. Giles Wright, *Afro-Americans in New Jersey: A Short History*, (New Jersey: New Jersey Historical Commission, 1988), 14.

17. Wright, 13.

18. Wright, 13.

19. Wright, 13.

20. See Yusuf Nurridin's, "African-American Muslims and the Question of Identity: Conflicts Between Traditional Islam, African Heritage and the American Way." unpublished paper at Medgar Evers College, Brooklyn, New York.

21. Nurridin.

22. Nurridin. For a more in-depth discussion read Yusuf Nuriddin's unpublished, but highly insightful paper. (see note 20) His thesis is that "Islam in the African American experience did not occur in a vacuum, but rather it was a well organized network comprised of men such as Edward Wilmot Blyden, Marcus Garvey, and Duse Ali, which constituted a network of internationally traveled intellectuals and activists who were responsible for the spread of religious and anti-colonial ideas throughout the African American community."

23. The Ahmadiyyah Movement in Islam originated in India. In the first half of the 20th century (beginning in 1921), many African American Muslim communities were influenced by the mission of Indian Ahmadis to the United States. See McCloud's *African American Islam* for more information, 18.

24. Tony Martin, *Race First,* (Dover, Mass.: The Majority Press, 1986), 76.

25. Documented in Tony Martin's book, *Race First.*

26. Noble Drew Ali. *Holy Koran of the Moorish Science Temple*

27. Hadith is the second source from which the teachings of Islam are drawn. Hadith literally means a saying conveyed to man, but in Islamic terminology Hadith means sayings of the Prophet Muhammad, his action or practice of his silent approvalof the action or practice. Hadith and Sunnah are used interchangeably, but sometimes these are used for different meanings, states Dr. Khalid Alvi.

28. Some researchers have said that Noble Drew Ali traveled to the Arabian Peninsula and to many North African countries. If this is true, it seems highly improbable that he did not have access to the primary sources of Islam, namely, the Qur'an and Hadiths. One important challenge for researchers is to uncover and document the facts connected to Drew Ali's alleged travels abroad.

29. Heshaam Jaaber, interview by author, Elizabeth, NJ June 1997.

30. The term dawah in this context means to invite to Islam; to discuss with others about its truthfulness.

31. I recommend this book to researchers interested in the connection between West African Islamic cultural retentions in the New World. Also, Diouf's book is a compliment to Allan Austin's *African Muslims Enslaved in Antebellum America.*

32. Nobel Drew Ali, "Moorish Literature" (no date or place of publication), 12.

33. Walter Elliot, "Newark's Moorish-Americans Continue," *Visions Metro Weekly*, Jan 13–19, 2006, 7.

34. McCloud, *African-American Islam*, 13.

35. Noble Drew Ali, "Moorish Literature" (no date or place of publication), 10.

36. Ali, "Moorish Literature," 6.

37. McCloud, *African-American Islam*, 15.

38. Clement Price, "The Afro-American Community in Newark" Ph.D. Diss., 85.

39. Claude Andrew Clegg III. *An Original Man: The Life and Times of Elijah Muhammad*, (New York: St Martin's Press, 1997),19.

40. Clegg III, *An Original Man*, 19.

41. Heshaam Jaaber, Interview by author, Elizabeth, NJ June 1997.

42. Angela Y. Walton-Raji, "Black Indian Genealogy Research: African-American Ancestors Among the Five Civilized Tribes," compiled by Jehadi Islaamic Educational Institute, Elizabeth, New Jersey. Allan Austin's *African Muslims in Antebellum America: Transatlantic Stories and Spiritual Struggles* also sheds light on the phenomenon of African Muslim and Native American encounters in the West. Researchers may also find useful the book, *Black Indians,* by William Katz.

43. Ravanna Bey, "The Moorish-American Prophet Noble Drew Ali," *The Universal Truth* Vol 2, No 3, 5.

44. Ravanna Bey.

45. Ravanna Bey.

46. See Introduction to Stanley Lane-Poole's, *The Story of the Moors in Spain*.

47. For an in-depth discussion of the early African presence in early America see Dr. Ivan Van Sertima's, *They Came Before Columbus* and also his other well documented study, *African Presence in Early America*. Researchers may also find helpful, Dr. Abdullah Hakim Quick's book, *Deeper Roots: Muslims in the America's and the Caribbean From Before Columbus to the Present*, Ta-Ha Publications, London, 1996.

48. Prince A. Farad, "Moorish Science History," *The Universal Truth* 2, No 3 G., (Stone Mountain, Georgia).

49. Prince A. Farad, "Moorish Science History." E.U. Essien-Udom also mentioned this in his excellent study, *Black Nationalism: A Search For an Identity in America,* University of Chicago Press. See page 34. However, he did not specify which American President.

50. Allan Austin, *African Muslims in Antebellum America: Transatlantic Stories and Spiritual Struggles*, (New York: Routledge, 1997), 14.

51. Austin, *African Muslims in Antebellum America,* 14.

52. Austin, 11.

53. The term *bi'da* is an *Arabic* word meaning religious innovation. Many *ahadith* affirm that bi'da is something that should be despised by all Muslims because it introduces into the religion that which was not sanctioned by the Prophet Muhammad (saw).

54. See Hakim Sabree and Ayesha K. Mustafaa's article titled "Revolution Starts in the Culture," *Muslim Journal*, December 23, 1994.

55. Sulayman S. Nyang, "Islam in the United States of America: A Review of the sources" 171 Also, the reader should be mindful that these works in many respects are removed from the universal spirit of Islam.

56. In Sulayman Nyang's article, "Islam in the United States of America: A Review of the Sources," he mentions something useful to researchers concerning the tensions that have existed between immigrant and indigenous Muslims. I quote: "Though the organizers of the First Islamic Conference of North America [which took place in Newark, NJ in 1977] were most likely not too receptive to the black nationalist element in the Ansar teachings, they were however willing to welcome them as

fellow Muslims in the Sunni Muslim Jammaah in the United States of America. The above mentioned point is quite significant when we take note of the fact that the Ansars have stated over and over again in their literature, that the Pakistani Moslem and the so-called Arab Moslem have not measured up to their responsibilities and the expectations of the Afro-American Muslim population. In the view of the Ansars, the arrival of their leader has put an end to the need for guidance from these other Muslims and hence truth will no longer be kept from them."

57. A thob is a form of religious clothing resembling a long dress usually worn by Muslim men.

58. Farad, "Moorish Science History."

59. Adib Rashad (James Miller), *Elijah Muhammad & The Ideological Foundation of the Nation of Islam,* (Hampton, Virginia: U.B. & U.S. Communications Systems, 1994), 68. This is a good book, with contributions from Dr. Alauddin Shabazz, Dr. Na'im Akbar, Dr. Dorothy Blake Fardan, Dr. Sulayman Nyang and H. Khalif Khalifah.

60. Farad, *The Universal Truth*, 12–13.

61. Darlene Hine, *The African-American Odyssey*, vol. 1: to 1877, (Upper Saddle River, NJ: Prentice Hall), 103.

62. Darlene Hine, 105.

Chapter Four

New Direction

MUHAMMAD EZALDEEN AND THE ADDEYNU ALLAHE UNIVERSAL ARABIC ASSOCIATION (AAUAA)

Among those correspondents who have been prepared by the General Centre [World Youngmen Muslim Association in Cairo, Egypt] to be a good nucleus to preach for Islam in their countries, we quote, as an example, three Muslims from the heart of America and Africa . . . The first is the American Mohammed EzzEl Din, who came to Egypt in 1931 escaping racial oppression. He embraced Islam, and stayed in the hospitality and good care of the General Centre for five years. In America, he became an eminent preacher for Islam . . . [The second was an European American, Abdel-Rahman Lutz, who came to Cairo from California in 1947, and an African named Kabin-Kaba from Senegal who came to Cairo in 1945.][1]

The Addenynu Allahe Universal Arabic Association was the first organized Sunni Muslim presence in Newark. It began in 1941 at 95 Prince Street with the founding of a chapter of the Addeynu Allahe Universal Arabic Association (AAUAA) by Mohammed Ezaldeen. Professor Ezaldeen, as he is fondly referred to by two of his former students Heshaam Jaaber and Musa Hamad, is believed to have been born in the United States of America during the early part of the twentieth century. Dennis Walker, in his book *Islam and the Search for African-American Nationhood* stated that "Ezaldeen, formerly Lomax Bey, had been one of the members of the original Moorish Temple of 1913 in Newark."[2] According to scant records available to me, the AAUAA was incorporated in the state of New Jersey on August 5, 1938. During the 1940s and 50s, as was stated, this organization played a major role in the establishment of an Islamic community in Newark. Today, its national headquarters is located at Muhammad Ezaldeen Village, Cedar Avenue, Elm, New Jersey. Although its influence in the area has declined, it is to this organization's credit that the emerging Sunni Muslim community in Newark had a clear and identifiable base. It is the parent organization of many Sunni groups in the Greater Newark area. In fact, a number of Sunni Muslim groups that emerged in the city owe intellectual heritage to Ezaldeen and the AAUAA. Among the later organizations that were direct offshoots of the AAUAA are Masjid Deenul-Lah, Baitul Khaliq and Baitul Quraish.

In 1941, the year that the AAUAA became recognized in Newark, the event preceded the establishment of the Nation of Islam (NOI) in the area at the first major Temple in Newark about 1959. Although both groups had a presence in the area, the Nation of Islam, during the turbulent 1960s, became greater in numbers, partly due to its recruitment style, the attention given to it by the national media, the charisma of Malcolm X, the social conditions in the African American community and the tacit reputation of Elijah Muhammad. In contrast, the AAUAA was for the most part a low profile group that did not receive a great deal of media attention. Some believe that it was because Professor Ezaldeen, the organization's founder, attempted to teach an interpretation of Is-

AAUAA members at social gathering in Newark. (Courtesy of Wahab Arbubakar.)

lam that placed emphasis on the study of Arabic and the primary sources of Islam, namely the Qur'an and the Sunnah. After Ezaldeen died in 1957 the members continued his low key style of teaching.

As most African American Muslims know, Elijah Muhammad was not in favor of giving his followers the freedom to study the primary sources because in his view, such was not appropriate for the immediate needs of the African-American community. In response to the question of whether there was tension between the AAUAA and the NOI because of this, Heshaam Jaaber stated "there has always been tension, but it wasn't tension in the sense of opposition or hostility.' 'The Nation always preached about the Honorable Elijah Muhammad; we didn't, we promoted the Sunnah. 'Also, the reason we didn't have that problem was because Mr. Elijah Muhammad had said don't mess with the Sunnis because he was out of the Moors."[3] Thus, it was the AAUAA's insistence on promoting the orthodox views that made its program different from the NOI as well as that of the MSTA. For most of the twentieth century, the numbers of the Sunni community in Newark, comparatively speaking, was small. However, the irony of it all is that the majority of those who identify with Islam in the Greater Newark area today would classify themselves as Sunni Muslims. This is largely due to conversion, since most in the area are first and second generation Muslims.

AAUAA women pioneers. (Courtesy of Wahab Arbubakar.)

HAMETIC (BLACK) ARABS

In the organization's scant literature, Ezaldeen is described as being born of
Hametic Arab parentage. Hametic was the term he used to describe African
Americans. He believed and taught that African Americans were descendants
of the original Arabs. Thus, Ezaldeen like Drew Ali taught his followers to be
proud of their Afro-Asiatic heritage. Rather than placing emphasis on the
study of ancient African history and culture as many of the cultural nationalist and Afro-centric groups did, Ezaldeen linked his community to ancient
Arabia. This reality was recognized by the poet, militant playwright and social activist, Amiri Baraka (formerly LeRoi Jones), who stated in his autobiography that "the two influences, orthodox Islam and the African-derived cultural nationalism, had to clash and they did.[4] "The Sunnis were not very
advanced politically," Baraka stated. They said that blacks were really Arabs,
that the true Arab was black. Arab means black, but they were very derogatory about Africa and things African."[5] Talib, a former AAUAA member
stated, "at the time, the question of identity was an issue . . . the African
American was not unified to a great degree . . . thus, when you became a part
of the Addeynu Allahe Universal Arabic Association, one of the things it
taught you was about your national heritage . . . that heritage was said to have
mostly been from the Arab nation . . . they tried to make us different from the
Afro-American at that time who were not unified . . . These were up against
those who wished to push more for the freedom of blacks . . . So they said
that we were Arab Americans and that we really didn't fit in with the Afro
American movement at that time . . . Further, they (black American non Muslims) believed mostly in Christianity and we believed in Allah. In a short explanation of how the term Hametic Arab came about, Professor Ezaldeen referring in large part to Biblical history as well as some of the statements made
by Noble Drew Ali in his *Holy Koran of the Moorish Science Temple*, stated:

> We Hametic Arabs are descendants of the first Arabs: Nebajoth Kedar, Adbel,
> Mibsam, Mishma, Dumah, Massa, Hadar, Tema, Jetur, Naphish, and Kedamah
> the twelve sons of Isma'al (Upon him be peace) whose father and mother were
> Ibrahim and Hagar. Ibrahim (Upon him be peace) was a Prophet and our Royal
> mother (Hagar) was a princess from the house of Pharaoh. Through Hagar
> (Upon her be peace) we trace our heritage through Kush (Ethiopia), Phut
> Mizraim (Egypt) and Canan then through Ham, son of Noah. Through Ibrahim
> (Upon him be peace) we trace our heritage through Ham, son of Noah. Every
> nation has a mother and a father. Allah says in his Qur'an, he has made us of na-
> tions and tribes so that we may know one another and the best of us is the one
> most pious! (al-Quran 49:13) We are not a Black race, nor an African race nor a
> Negro or Colored race. We are a nation of Arabs, who are Olive-Skinned—a na-

tion Honorable, Noble and Upright and owe our existence to the Almighty, Powerful, Allah (The Most High).[6]

STRUGGLE FOR BLACK LIBERATION

Further, we learn from Heshaam Jaaber that one of the main objectives of the orthodox Muslim community from which he sprang was to keep alive the debate concerning the anti-colonial nature of the black liberation struggle. Following in the path of his predecessors Garvey, Drew Ali and Ezaldeen, Jaaber would oft-times link the struggle of African American Muslims to the struggle of not only Muslims in other parts of the world, but also to that of blacks throughout the world. Just as Malcolm had publicly acknowledged his desire to see Islam as a possible solution to the race problem and social ills in American society upon returning from his second Hajj in 1964, Jaaber was known for recommending Islam as a source of guidance for the black liberation struggle.

> I used to go over to the Spirit House [in Newark in the 1960s]. Over there was a rebellion against the onslaughts and violations of civil and human rights. I used to go over there because they were advocating revolution. But, when I got there, I found that there were a lot of young people, and that they didn't really know what to teach. Of course, I started teaching Islam because I knew that that would take them through, and that it would hook them up on the national. And, when I explained this to LeRoi Jones, he became a Muslim. I named him Ameer Barakat. In Swahili, it's Baraka. I also named his wife, Amina, and gave them both Shahada.[7]

These statements by Jaaber are validated by Baraka who also stated in his autobiography the following:

> I met the tall, slender, beautifully dark-skinned Heesham, Hajj Heesham, signifying that he had made "the Hajj," the journey to Mecca required of all Muslims . . . It was Heesham who gave me the name Ameer Barakat (the Blessed Prince). Sylvia was named Amina (faithful) after one of Muhammad's wives. Later, under Karenga's influence I changed my name to Amiri, Bantuizing or Swahilizing the first name and the pronunciation of the last name as well.[8]

ISLAM: A VIABLE ALTERNATIVE TO BLACK-NATIONALISM

Heshaam Jaaber, only one of Ezaldeen's most prominent students, stated that "the curriculum of the Addeynu Allahe Universal Arabic Association was similar to that of one who studied in college doing their undergraduate studies."⁹ Ezaldeen's program was a religious studies program that was designed to uplift the spirit and educate. For Jaaber, 95 Prince Street, Newark, was a place that he would go to learn about the fundamentals of Islam. He seemed to have had a special pride in the fact that his first Islamic teacher, Professor Ezaldeen, was a formally educated man of African ancestry. It was through Ezaldeen that he learned how to fulfill the duties of an Imam. In addition to teaching the people about the fundamentals of Islam, Jaaber's duties as Imam included leading the community in performing the five daily prayers, delivering the Friday *khutbah* (sermon) and leading the congregational prayer, performing marriage ceremonies, funerals services, and Eids (Muslim festivals after Ramadan and in commemoration of Prophet Ibrahim's willingness to sacrifice his son for God). Because the Eid celebrations grew to be large, Addeynu oft-times had to rent space in a large enough hall to accommodate the many Muslim families that desired to engage in the Eid prayers and festivities. Annual gatherings around July fourth would also take place and the AAUAA could expect many visitors at them. Oft-times, Eids were held at Scott Beauty School in the old Kruger building on High and Court Street.

Not much has been discovered about Ezaldeen's early life. Like Drew Ali, some of the AAUAA elders believe that he was among those who migrated to Newark from the South, probably during the time of the Great Migration. Others say he was originally from the Philadelphia, Pennsylvania area. But, in light of some of the background information that we do have on him, it seems that he was destined to become the religious teacher and theologian that he became. The stories surrounding his early days as a young boy are very similar to the ones told about Drew Ali. "Upon completion of his high school education in the United States, he was said to have traveled and studied abroad, like Drew Ali, in countries such as Morocco, Libya, Egypt, and several other African countries." "His last formal educational experience was said by some to have been in Turkey.' In 1930, under the name of Ali Mohammed Bey he arrived in Turkey, and delivered a petition to Kemal Ataturk on behalf of 28,000 Negroes facing prejudice in America, requesting that his sect be allowed to found a colony in Anatolia, Angora or any other under-populated farming area."¹⁰ As a mark of distinction, the organization's scant literature states that he was the holder of the highest honor given by the oldest organized seat of learning in the Islamic world, Cairo's 1000 year old, Al-Azhar University's Maulana Al-Azhar Degree. (Said to be equivalent to the Western world's Ph.D.)" This alleged accomplishment is questionable, however, since we have no clear evidence that Ezaldeen attended Al-Azhar University. One source states that before he converted to Islam, "Ezaldeen had been a Christian Minister in Pennsylvania whose congregation had sent him to Rome to further his education . . . he then met a man who encouraged him to study Islam in Egypt."[11] Professor Amir Al-Islam of Medgar Evers College described Ezaldeen as a towering figure in African American Sunni Islam. "One of the first African Americans to master the Arabic language and Islamic Studies in Egypt, professor Ezaldeen, upon his return to the states, rejected the teachings of the Moorish Science Temple and developed orthodox Islamic communities in several cities throughout the U.S. . . . In addition, [Ezaldeen] was responsible for establishing the first national Islamic organization among Sunni Muslims, the United Islamic Communities, which included among others, Shaikh Dawud, members of the First Cleveland and Pittsburgh Mosques."[12]

Upon his arrival back to the United States in 1936, Ezaldeen started a Muslim community in Buffalo New York, which came to be known as Ezaldeen Village. He then started an extension of this in South Jersey, after successfully purchasing some land there back in the late 1930s. It was from this base that he had eventually extended the influence of the organization all the way into Newark. Before he moved the headquarters to Newark, it was common for Muslims from Newark to visit the site in South Jersey. Wahab Arbubakar, an elder of the community and a Newark resident, was among them. Arbubakar was among the pioneers who assisted with the project on Prince Street. When Arbubakar came to Newark in 1946, he did not know much about Islam. He recalled that one had to make three meetings before he could join the organization. Arbubakar stated, "when I met Professor Ezaldeen, he spoke about the one true Allah, and the prophets and the holy books; he also spoke about the hereafter." Further, he states, "the most profound thing that I heard was the *al fatiha*[13] and the call to prayer. When he told us the meaning, it had a tremendous effect on me; especially when he translated it and explained it to us."[14] As Arbubakar told the story, the spirit moved him to call the *adhan* (the Muslim call to prayer) in a melodious tone as this interview was being conducted.

Ezaldeen endeavored to establish a national Islamic movement as early as the late 1940s. On March 20, 1949, from his Newark headquarters, he sent a letter to Buffalo, New York beckoning the pioneers to organize themselves around orthodox Islamic principles. He stated:

As the founder, the Supreme President, and President of the National Assembly, I deem it necessary to write this letter of information that it may encourage the new members and also that it may be a reminder to the Pioneers. This organization is both Religious and National. This unit at Buffalo was chartered at Albany, New York October 29, 1938 by an Executive Committee. The Executive Committee has the same power of the State National Assembly, before it is organized. When a by-law is proposed by the Executive Committee and presented to the members and it receives the majority votes, such by-law become a State National Law, so long as it does not conflict with the laws of the National Assembly. No person is eligible to become a member or to hold an official post except he or she prays with the members. Even the King must pray with the members of Al-Islam. This I know prayer can be made anywhere something clear is spreaded down, except in the toilet, all wood and ground are holy. Sin appears when people of filthy hearts and minds bow on them.[15]

The Brotherhood of Islam in Philadelphia was a part of the AAUAA as well. Also, the first organization even before the AAUAA came into existence was the United Islamic Society. Muslims in this organization were stretched out as far as Florida. Also, as part of this association, there was the first Mosque of Pittsburgh.[16]

NOTES

1. *The General Centre World Young Men Muslims Association*, Cairo United Arab Republic (Atlas Press 11, 13, Souk el Tewfikia, Cairo Tel, 40797).

2. Dennis Walker, *Islam and the Search for African-American Nationhood*, (Altanta, Georgia: Clarity Press, 2005), 244. This is an interesting find. Ezaldeen more than likely returned to Newark when allegedly he was denied a charter in Philadelphia upon returning from Egypt.

3. Heshaam Jaaber, Interview by author, Elizabeth, NJ, June 1997. In my interview with Jaaber he shared that a relative of the Muhammad family told him that Elijah was once affiliated with the Moors. Nevertheless, there is quite a bit of controversy concerning this notion that Elijah Muhammad may have been affiliated with the Moors. Ravanna Bey in *Universal Truth* vol. 2, no. 3 p. 6 makes an interesting assertion suggesting that Farad Muhammad, Elijah's mentor, protested the authority of John givens El when he claimed to be the reincarnation of Noble Drew Ali upon his death. Farad and another fellow named Mealy El later went on to establish their own Moorish Science Temples. Farad, also referred to at that time as Professor Ford, converted one of the Detroit Moorish Temples to his own Temple of the Lost-Found people of Islam. As is well known, Elijah Muhammad was a convert of Farad. When Farad returned to the Middle East, Elijah assumed leadership and changed the name to Allah's Temple of Islam. The implication here, it seems to me, is that Elijah was not connected to the Moors, although his mentor, Farad, was.

4. Amiri Baraka, *The Autobiography of LeRoi Jones (Amiri Baraka)*, New York: Freundlich Books, 1984.), 273.

5. Baraka, *The Autobiography*, 273.

6. [Addeynu Allahe Universal Arabic Association Inc.?] "History," (photocopy). This brief history of the AAUAA was shared by Wahab ArbuBakar.

7. Jaaber, interview, 1997.

8. Baraka, *The Autobiography*, 267.

9. Jaaber, interview, 1997.

10. Walker, *Islam and the Search for African-American Nationhood*, 243.

11. Abdullah Hakim Quick, *Deeper Roots*: Muslims in the Americas and the Caribbean From Before Columbus to the Present, (London: Ta-Ha Publishers Ltd., 1996), 9.

12. Amir Al-Islam, "Beyond Malcolm: Muslim Leadership for the 21st Century," *The Message*, Sept-Oct 1996, 28.

13. The *al fatiha* is the opening chapter of the Qur'an.

14.vWahab Arbubakar, "Interview by author," 30 November 1997.

15. A letter from Ezaldeen to the members of the AAUAA

16. Jaaber, interview, 97.

Women of Baitul Quraish.

Imam Wahy Deen Shareef of Masjid Warithideen in Irvington, NJ, is a Senior Advisor to Newark Mayor Cory Booker. Here, Imam Shareef addresses the audience at a Newark in Transition Community Meeting held at the Paul Robeson Center at Rutgers Newark.

Reverend William Howard, (Far right.) Pastor of Bethany Baptist Church, and Imam Wahy Deen Shareef (middle) at a City of Newark sponsored community meeting held at the Paul Robeson Center. (Photo by Author.)

(left to right) Imam Wahy Deen Shareef, Craig Drinkard, and other participants involved in the series of community meetings sponsored by Mayor Cory Booker. (Photo by Author.)

Rashad El-Amin of Masjid Al-Haqq gives a presentation on the relationship between Ramadan and good health at a pre-Ramadan Health Fair hosted by the West Side Park Community Center in Newark

Imam Dawud Abdul-Haqq of the National Islamic Association (NIA) listening to a speaker at the community health fair held at Westside Park Community Center

Matina Ismail (right) speaks to Newark community resident about health at a UMDNJ and urban mosque sponsored community health fair hosted by Newark's Masjid Al-Haqq

Imam Abdul Akbar Muhammad (smiling with white cufi on) of Newark's Masjid Ali Muslim enjoys social time with members of his congregation after Eid Prayer

Branford Place. (Photo by Author.)

Branford Place Merchant and Pioneer, Abdul-Karim (right). (Photo by Author.)

Face painting (Sunah Nash and Yasmine Muhammad).

Valley Nadira Nash, owner and director of the Talib Academy and Talib Learning Center with Sunah (left) and Shomari (right) with striped shirt during Eid festivities.

Brothers Muhsin and Salim (right) embrace at a program held at Essex County College in remembrance of the contributions of the Nation of Islam in the city of Newark.

Dr. Ned Wilson, Professor Michael Nash and Dr. Clement Price pose for a picture before Nash's presentation at the Library of Congress on "Public Space, Muslims and the Urban Mosque in Newark, NJ History."

Professor Michael Nash and Dr. Lenworth Gunther at the Essex County College Faculty Retirement Dinner in April of 2006.

Michael Nash's remarks at faculty retirement dinner honoring Dr. Lenworth Gunther

Thank you very much for asking me to say a few words on behalf of Dr. Lenworth Gunther.

Over 30 years of service has enabled Dr. Lenworth Gunther to set a precedent (as the people's historian) in the Greater Newark Community and in the state of NJ. His legacy as a scholar/historian within our midst is well-known and will go down in history as a model of excellence for all aspiring historians and academicians.

What is truly remarkable about Lenny is not his superior oratorical skills or even his vast knowledge of history, which are well known, but rather the spirit behind the man that has enabled him to impact the lives of so many people. His commitment to the empowerment of the disadvantaged and understudied groups in our society will too go down in history as a model of excellence for all to emulate. Lenny's courage, over the years, to educate himself and others about the pertinent (even controversial) issues in our society is beyond reproach. His conviction to create open forums, with the academician as part in parcel of the community at-large (not separate from it), is a standard of excellence that exemplifies the true role of the academician.

So without further due, it gives me great pleasure to introduce Dr. Lenworth Gunther.

Chapter Five

Continuities and Linkages

THE LINK BETWEEN THE MOORISH SCIENCE TEMPLE, ADDEYNU ALLAHE UNIVERSAL ARABIC ASSOCIATION, THE NATION OF ISLAM AND GLOBAL ISLAM

Some have expressed doubts, but it is clear that Ezaldeen knew Noble Drew Ali of the Moorish Science Temple and was certainly connected to the organization before he left the U.S. to study abroad. Some have said that Ezaldeen was influenced by Noble Drew Ali's movement and at one point served as a minister in the early stages of the Moorish Science Temple of America.[1] Walker documents that James Lomax Bey—Ezaldeen's Moorish name—had been head of a flourishing Moorish Temple in Detroit prior to leaving the U.S. for his studies in Egypt beginning in 1931. This could explain why when Ezaldeen founded his AAUAA in Newark in 1938 he was not intimidated or discouraged as a result of the Moorish-American presence there. His prior experience with the group had prepared him for what he would find in Newark. Walker stated:

> In 1929, Lomax had challenged the authority of the Noble Drew Ali, partly over funds. Governor J. Lomax Bey had built up Temple #4 in Detroit into one of the largest in the movement, with 1500 members and four businesses—two grocery shops, a laundry and a printing press. By March 1929, Lomax was claiming that Prophet Drew Ali had no more power and that the finance from Detroit should be in his charge: he would send none on to Prophet Drew. He had yelled defiance to Drew's face before over 1,000 people on February 15, 1929 so the Prophet had issued a letter booting him out. It was at this point that Lomax changed his name to Ali Mohammed Bey.[2]

One publication, *The Universal Truth*, identifies Ezaldeen as one of the MSTA directors when the organization was first incorporated in 1926. "According to various government records, listed as directors were Drew Ali, James Lomax,[3] Johnny Renyolds, Eddie Watts and Sammy Rucker; all of Chicago."[4] Further, the idea is not a far-fetched one since both Drew Ali and Ezaldeen had similar ideas, and used similar approaches in leading their respective communities in Newark.

Oral history also lends considerable support to the claim that there was a strong link between Ezaldeen and Drew Ali. Some former AAUAA members in hindsight recall that the AAUAA's Jumah services (congregational prayer services) were held on Sunday instead of Friday in the beginning stages. The Sunday meetings in the initial stages of the organization could have been influenced by the MSTA, which was known even to the present day to hold at least one of its congregational meetings on Sunday, probably because it was difficult to get people to attend the Temple on Friday. More than likely, Friday conflicted with work schedules and made it difficult for those interested to hear the new message. Also it has been reported that the AAUAA members during the early stages of the organizations development used chairs in the prayer area at the Prince Street location. Interestingly, both the AAUAA and the MSTA used the term olive-skinned to describe African Americans because this term is used in Bible scripture to describe the righteous people of God. Also, with respect to genealogy, both Drew Ali and Ezaldeen depended upon the Old Testament to trace the tribal lineage of modern blacks. Biblical and Qur'anic Prophets such as Noah and Abraham were revered by them both. The significance of Noah was that he was the father of Ham, who was said to be the father of black/African peoples.[5] Also, both organizations saw the holy city of Mecca as a sacred place and stated this in much of their literature. An important difference, however, is that the AAUAA eventually encouraged their members to strictly guard the practice of the five pillars of Islam, while the MSTA did not. Thirdly, members of both organizations wore the red fez (a hat common to many Muslims in North Africa) as a symbol of distinction.[6] However, for AAUAA members, it was also common for some to wear other types of Islamic head gear. During the 1940s, it was common for people to see both Moorish Americans and Hamitic Arabs wearing the red fez in the Prince Street area. One of the AAUAA members of that period stated, "at the time we were all of the *taraboosh*, the red fez hat.' ' Most of us—that's what we wore—and that identified us—it set us apart from all of the other religious movements—and as people began to see us more they said here come the Muslims.[7] They did not identify us with the X's—they just said the Muslims, here come the Muslims." Fourthly, the houses of worship of both organizations were called temples rather than mosques or masjids.

Apparently, both leaders understood that for political purposes it would not be expedient to attempt to attract African Americans to the new faith by using Arabic terms that they were not familiar with, so they continued to use the term temple. Also the term temple may have attracted less attention from the greater Christian community, and therefore less open hostility. Fifthly, Ezaldeen was fondly referred to by his followers as Professor Ezaldeen. Some sources state that Drew Ali was known to have used the title of Professor as well. Isa Muhammad, in one of his pamphlets, stated that Noble Drew Ali was also known as Professor Drew, the Egyptian Adept.[8] Also, both leaders placed great emphasis on discovering their national origins. Their followers were given lessons about their tribal lineage and ancient heritage which was said to have begun in ancient Africa, a land known to have been ruled by blacks. Few historians today refute the idea of the relationship between black Africans and the highly developed civilizations in ancient Africa. Cheikh Anta Diop, a Senegalese scholar, speaks extensively about this relationship in his classic study, *The African Origins of Civilization: Myth or Reality*. Dr. Diop's main thesis is that historical, archeological, and anthropological evidence supports the theory that the civilization of ancient Egypt, the first that history records, was actually Negroid in origin. Also, both emphasized to their followers that they should respect the American flag. The general train of thought at that time was to be physically in America, but not of its materialistic and morally degenerative culture. Unlike Elijah Muhammad's Nation of Islam, neither the MSTA nor the AAUAA after Ezaldeen's encounter with Turkish officials in 1929 expressed any desire to emigrate out of the country.[9] Finally, both Ezaldeen and Drew Ali tried to use Islamic principles to eradicate the germ of ethnocentric arrogance from the hearts of their followers, an approach espoused and promoted later by El-Hajj Malik El-Shabazz after his historic and widely popularized hajj (pilgrimage) to Mecca.

Malcolm X, reportedly, had debated a Rutgers Sociology professor in 1961 at the Rutgers-Newark campus apparently representing the philosophy of Elijah Muhammad and the NOI. When Malcolm X returned to the U.S. from the Hajj in 1964, however, he affirmed publicly that his pilgrimage had broadened his scope and blessed him with a new insight on the issue of race. The true Islam, he stated, had shown him that a blanket indictment of all white people was as wrong as when whites made blanket indictments against all blacks. Many have lamented that Malcolm had known about true Islam even before the Hajj through conversations he had had with Elijah's second youngest son, Wallace. Apparently, Malcolm was also friendly with those who were students of Ezaldeen or influenced in some way by his teachings. Members of the Newark-based Council of the Brothers, although influenced by Elijah's NOI, used to sit down regularly with Muhammad

Ezaldeen when he used to teach Islam on Prince Street because they regarded him as a learned man in the religion.[10] Malcolm as early as the 1950s was in contact with some of them through a joint effort to establish a radio program.[11] The project apparently did not materialize, but the indirect influence of Ezaldeen on Malcolm through these encounters is another interesting development for historians to examine. It should also be understood that, Malcolm's mentor, Elijah Muhammad had followers in Newark even though a formal Temple had not been established until the early 1960s. In 1943, the *New Jersey Herald* published a story informing its readership about the existence in the state of seven members from the Allah Temple of Islam (The Allah Temple of Islam was founded by Farad Muhammad in Detroit after the death of Noble Drew Ali. After Farad disappeared, Elijah assumed leadership) who had been arrested for draft evasion.[12] This suggests that Elijah Muhammad's influence in Newark, too, goes back as far as the early 1940s. Elijah also wrote about some experiences he had in Newark. He stated, "in Newark they (meaning the Moorish-Americans) rejected me twice . . . one of their brothers followed me out there in Newark and he said, "I just wish I were the Sheik, I would let you teach all night because you were telling us things we never heard; I know it is the truth but our Sheik is so narrow about it that he doesn't want to hear you say anything . . . but that is who we want to say something; the one who knows more than we." Elijah said, "That is the way it should be."[13] So it is clear that all three men, Drew Ali, Ezaldeen and Elijah were active in Newark for sure in the early 1940s and were successful in setting the stage in that city for what became an influx of Islam influenced people from the three streams of consciousness that their leaders represented. What also seems clear is that both Ezaldeen and Elijah were quite aware of the work that the Moors had done in Newark popularizing Islam. So by the time that Malcolm X had made his Hajj and returned as Malik Shabazz in 1964, foreign Muslims through such people as Farad Muhammad, Mohammed Ezaldeen and another interesting figure not previously mentioned, Sati Majid[14] had not only known about these early movements, but knew that the United States of America had become a place ripe for the propagation of Islam. Malik Shabazz's public confessions about his life changing experience in Mecca was recognized and honored by an affiliate of the organization that Ezaldeen received his Islamic education from. A pamphlet of the General Centre World Young Men Muslims Association quoted Malcolm as saying the following:

There were tens of thousands of pilgrims from all over the world. They were all colors, from blue-eyed blonds to black-skinned Africans, but were all participating in the same ritual, displaying a spirit of unity and brotherhood that my experiences in America had led me to believe could never exist between white and non-white.[15]

Malik Shabazz had made such an impression on Arab Muslim officials that one of their Ambassadors in America wrote, "if we had spent a million dollars to preach for Islam, we could not have reached the impression made by this man in the American community."[16] "Another Arab Ambassador said, "The conversion of Malcolm reminds me of Omar when he embraced Islam. Malcolm will surely be the Omar of the black Americans."[17] Malcolm in turn expressed his appreciation and gratitude to one prominent Arab Muslim official. He stated:

> I am most grateful to Dr. Mahmoud Youssef Shawarbi, Director of the Islamic Center of New York, for helping me to understand true Islam, a religion that teaches brotherhood and tolerance between peoples of all colors and national origins. He was instrumental in opening my eyes to Islam's views concerning cooperation between peoples in solving mutual problems amicably. He always reminded me of the relevant verse in our Holy [Quran] which says: Call unto the way of the Lord with wisdom and fair exhortation and reason with them in the better way. 16:125[18]

Elijah Muhammad's son, Wallace, D. Muhammad, would also follow in Malcolm's tradition and gradually reinforce this new universalistic teaching on the members of the NOI after his father died in 1975. It has been said that Imam W. Deen, not long after his rise to power in the Nation of Islam, from his Chicago headquarters, via satellite hook up, gave lectures on the universality of Islam and several shahadas[19] at one time at the historic NOI Mosque on South Orange Avenue.[20] The universal message of Islam he shared during those times was not new, but as Imam Mustafa El-Amin stated, "it was new [in some sense] to the members of the NOI"[21] who had for so long been led to believe in a radical idea that glorified black superiority.

In fact, the Nation of Islam, an off-shoot of the MSTA, is perhaps the most well known and best example that illustrates the desire for African Americans of the twentieth century influenced by Islam to adopt an idea—though un-Islamic—of black superiority. This tendency for charismatic African Americans influenced by Islam to identify themselves and other blacks as being Allah's chosen people in the early part of the 20th century is well known in the African American Muslim community and consequently has caused some discomfort and tension between the various groups as well as challenges for students of Muslim American history. It is useful once again to quote Professor Amir Al-Islam who brings some clarity to the different sides of the controversy that exists in the African American Muslim community. In his cover story essay, "Beyond Malcolm" published in the *Message International*, he stated that "these charismatic leaders felt that in addition to a new religion, African Americans needed to develop racial pride and a positive sense of identity and self-worth which would enable them to move beyond the negative characterization of the "demonized other" which was promulgated by the greater society."[22] The NOI philosophy, which castigated European Americans as a race of white devils and African Americans as black gods is well known. It is important to understand that after Drew Ali died many Moorish Americans remained loyal to his teachings relative to race, refusing to accept many of the new concepts introduced to African Americans through the NOI teachings. However, a significant number of them did join the ranks of the Nation and declared Elijah Muhammad as the natural successor of Drew Ali. Others, again, found professor Ezaldeen and honored him and his teachings.

Noble Drew Ali's Moorish Science Temple had some direct influence on the ideas and organizational strategy of Muhammad Ezaldeen. According to another account by Professor Yusuf Nuruddin, Ezaldeen was a former member of the Moorish Science Temple whose Moorish name was Lomax Bey.[23] One thing for certain is that even the strategies used by both to attract native Newarkers were similar. Like Drew Ali, Ezaldeen taught that African Americans (whom he called Hametics or Hametic Arabs) were a part of a larger international community of Muslims, and that it was essential for them to rejoin, if not physically, at least mentally and spiritually, the world community of Muslims. Although the AAUAA did not specifically turn to Morocco, as did the MSTA, as a symbolic gesture of wanting to return to its roots, it did turn to the East with respect to styles of dress, language, diet, and customs. The organization held Muslim Africa in high regard.

The main difference between the two organizations, however, is that the AAUAA emphasized the importance of studying the Qur'an, learning the Arabic language, and becoming familiar with the hadith literature (traditions and sayings of the Prophet Muhammad). Also, while it was more common for MSTA members to attach the surname of Bey or El to their first name, AAUAA members did not adopt that practice. Another important point is that the AAUAA, unlike the MSTA, did not position itself as a secretive organization, nor did its leader Muhammad Ezaldeen claim to be a Prophet ordained by Allah. To Ezaldeen's credit, this change represents the first major shift in Muslim community development, one which brought Newark's African Americans who studied Islam closer to its universal teachings. In fact, it was through Ezaldeen's influence that these African Americans began to use the common terminology, *al-Islam*. In addition to having been a student of Islamic Studies in Egypt, Ezaldeen is reported to have been an accomplished public school teacher who was committed to the proper development of the Islamic community in the United States.[24]

Further, the quest to reconstruct an identity for the African American was a passion of Professor Ezaldeen. Although he did not use the Moorish American designation to describe and define his community, he believed strongly, like Drew Ali, that all Muslims should know and honor their tribal lineage. He placed importance on the idea that salvation for the Hametic (African American) people lay in the discovery by them of the tribe from which they sprung. It appears that this is what separated his approach of propagating the religion from many of the foreign Muslim missionaries who too became active in the U.S. Indeed, there was a rather large Arab population he encountered when he was in Detroit, the city that had the largest concentration of Arabs in the U.S.A. But, more importantly, Ezaldeen introduced an entirely new spirit into the African American Islamic movement, a spirit that was deeply rooted in Islamic orthodoxy.

At this point in the study, it is useful to digress briefly to illustrate a common mood of African Americans about the new faith, and the role that this mood had in shaping their Muslim identity. The mindset of the many African Americans who embraced Islam in those years is probably very much typified by Shaykh Gani, another early member of AAUAA and the former Imam of Jabul Arabiyya in West Valley, New York. In explaining his Islamic renaissance to Bob Boyer in an interview with the Buffalo Evening News, August 15, 1987, he said:

> I was born as David McDuffy. My father was a Methodist and my mother was Baptist. When I would tell my name, some people would kid me about being a black Irishman. That bothered me. I found out that before they were brought to America as slaves, the religion of Africans was Islam. So I found a preacher who taught us black steel workers about our heritage and the Muslim religion . . . and I changed my name.[25]

Another Newark pioneer who goes by the name Talib stated:

> There were many things that attracted me to Islam. At the time I had grown up mostly being a Christian, but I was always interested in religion and trying to seek out more, and Islam appealed to me at the time because it brought about a closeness of the brotherhood that you didn't find at the time in Christianity. So that was one of the things that appealed to me. Also, I was a student of history. I liked history. Some of the things that we studied in school concerning the great religions—one of those religions was Islam and one thing that stuck in my mind was that they called people to pray five times day. Being a country boy and working on the farm it dawned on me, well, how can you pray five times a day

when you have to work? (laughing) But, lo and behold when it became apart of me then I found that that was easy. I found that it wasn't as hard as I thought it was.[26]

Thus, in addition to learning the fundamental principles of the Islamic faith, these Muslim African American pioneers were taught heritage lessons, which together comprised an Islamic Studies program in one complete package. Thus, there was some degree of cultural nationalism evident in the way that Islam was introduced, but this type of nationalism, these pioneers believed, was the permissible type that was consistent with Islamic thought. It was permissible in the sense that it did not emphasize ethnic or racial identity over the broader Muslim identity. In fact, the early pioneers in Newark believed that it was a sinful act not to want to identify with one's tribe or nation. As proof for these claims, they would often admonish one another by reciting the Qur'anic verse which states, "Allah has created you into Nations and Tribes so that you may know one another, not that you may despise one another; the best of you in the sight of Allah is the one who is the most pious."[27] This verse indicates that, although Allah (God) made humans different, they are essentially still the same because of their human nature. Thus the AAUAA taught that our goal as humans is the same—to accept and learn from our differences, and to strive to win Allah's favor through our submitting to him. In short, the ultimate goal of the human being was to surrender to the will of God. This perspective was not only different from that of the Nation of Islam, which promoted the idea that different natures existed between black and white people, but arguably it was an inevitable revolutionary consciousness that took shape as a result of internalizing the concept of Tauhid, and adhering to the five pillars of Islam. From the point of view of the Nation of Islam at that stage in its development, it was not possible for white people to surrender to God's will, which is one of the reasons why the organization advocated complete separation from white society. Tahleeb Sayyed, the first president of the AAUAA, was interviewed in a *Courier Express* Newspaper feature on the organization in 1945. During that interview, he stated that "there is no question that the Jamaat[28] was established as an orthodox Muslim group not subscribing to heresy, false gods or prophets."[29] Further, Sayyed said, our religious duties called for five prayers daily; at sunrise, noon, mid-afternoon, sunset and in the evening. Friday is our sacred day with noon the time for prayer."[30]

Like the members of the Moorish Science Temple, those African Americans who came into the fold of the Addeynu Allahe Universal Arabic Association did not refer to themselves as Afro-American, Negro or Black. Such terms were considered inappropriate and limited in scope insofar as describing a people considered as being a part of Dar al Islam (the Islamic World). Further, these terms were not appropriate because they did not link African Americans to their lineage, or to their historical and Islamic cultural heritage. In response to the question of whether there was a foreign Muslim influence on the AAUAA, Malik Arbubakar, the son of the elder pioneer Wahab Arbubakar stated:

> Professor Ezaldeen, I recall, was not dictated to by any international Islamic influence. What you saw in Addeynu was basically based on his direction, his teachings. My father had a number of Muslim friends who would visit us, but Professor Ezaldeen was keen to pointing out that we were Hametic Arabs. He taught us what we needed to know what was in the Quran. And he taught us that it was not necessary to praise or look up to Muslims from overseas. He didn't disrespect or dislike them. He just told us that because they came from Arabia, did not give them any greater claim on al-Islam than we had. Professor Ezaldeen taught us to not pay to much attention to color, yet he was very cognizant of the fact that the European man had done us great harm in America.[31]

As is quite evident, Ezaldeen laid a strong foundation for the emergence of the Sunni Muslim community in Newark. It is obvious that his students were given specific instructions relative to their practice of the *Deen*. As it seems, these instructions were clearly that Muslims should be involved with trying to insure that justice in American society was not an abstract idea that could never be realized, but that to play an active role in preserving it was a duty of every American, including Muslim Americans. In a careful examination of key events in African American and Newark history, we find that members of the AAUAA community were often at the forefront of the struggle to establish social and political justice in American society. Few know of the sacrifices made by them to insure that Muslims guided by the Islamic faith in the Greater Newark Community were conscientious citizens and respected as such. A case in point is an event that occurred during the time of the assassination of Malcolm X. "On February 21, 1965, my phone rang . . . the message, Haj Malik El-Shabazz has been assassinated . . . my first words "from Allah we come, to Allah we shall return," stated Heshaam Jaaber.[32] Further, as Jaaber states in his book, *The Final Chapter: I Buried Malcolm-Haj Malik El Shabazz*, at the time we were all members of the oldest Sunnah Muslim organization in New Jersey, having national scope, the Addeynu Allahe Universal Arabic Association Inc. of which I was the national Imam . . . After calls to two of the national officials, Wahab Abu-Bakr and the late Abdullah Majeed, informing them of our intentions, I was given the green light . . . and we were off, first to be with our families and then to New York to fulfill the right Malik held over us and our duty to Allah . . . Initially, immigrant communities were reluctant to get involved because they had felt that Malcolm was not really a true Muslim due to his earlier affiliation with the Nation of Islam."[33] Other examples of conscientious behavior and service to civic life and civic responsibility include when the Addeynu Allahe Universal Arabic Association assisted in bringing order to the 1967 disturbance that occurred in Newark. This disturbance started with an incident of police brutality against a black taxicab driver by the name of John Smith. From the high-rise tower of Hayes Homes Housing Project, it was reported that Smith was dragged out of a police car and into the front door of the Forth Precinct Police Station. The Kerner Report led by Illinois Governor Otto Kerner stated:

> Jabber, a teacher of Arabic and the Qur'an at the Spirit House in Newark, he is a militant who impressed the mayor with his sense of responsibility. . . . Although Jaaber believed that certain people were sucking the life blood out of the community—"Count the number of taverns and bars in the Elizabeth port area and compare them with the number of recreation facilities"—he had witnessed the carnage in Newark and believed it could serve no purpose to have a riot. Two dozen of his followers, in red fezzes, took to the streets to urge order. He himself traveled about in a car with a bullhorn.[34]

Abdullah Yasin, the Amir of Newark Community Masjid Baytul Khaliq on Chancellor Ave states, "it is a fact that most of the U.S. Northeastern Orthodox Islamic Communities, going back thirty to sixty or more years, emanated from or were directly associated with the Addeynu Allahe Universal Arabic Association (AAUAA), which began under the Amirship of Professor Muhammad Ezaldeen."[35] Ezaldeen was successful in building a number of communities around the country. His influence extended into areas such as Hammington, New Jersey; Pittsburgh, Pennsylvania; Cleveland, Ohio; Tallahassee, Florida; Buffalo, New York and Newark, New Jersey. According to local long-time AAUAA members, he got his foundation basically in Newark. AAUAA members believe that Ezaldeen was not a native Newarker, but that like many other African Americans during the Great Depression he probably migrated to Newark from the South. This, however, has not been proven. And, in spite of the fact that his death certificate states that he was born in West Africa, former members believe that his wife, Karema Ezaldeen, (Ezaldeen's wife passed away in 1995; she lived in Newark) only wrote West Africa on the death certificate as a decoy. That he is not a native Newarker is a fact, but his actual place of origin is uncertain. Many who new Ezaldeen personally confirmed that he did not have a foreign accent and that culturally, his mannerisms were very much like American blacks. Hence, it is very possible that Ezaldeen may have been the first African American or Hametic, as he would have preferred to be called, to teach orthodox Islam to his own people and have a considerable impact on the growth and development of Sunni Islam in the African American community. Dennis Walker makes an interesting observation. He states,

> In the perspective of our new century, Ezaldeen stands tall among the leaders of the Islam-influenced stream in African-American identity; his efforts to combine international diplomacy, a distinct national business community within the U.S., and some Arabization in culture by those communities, show vision as well as resolve.[36]

Although there is some validity to the claim that Ezaldeen was once a member of the Moorish Science Temple of America, the evidence clearly indicates that he became disinterested in its philosophy. To whatever extent he was involved, this had ceased by 1931, the year he began studying in Egypt after his apparent stint in Turkey. The evidence suggests that when he returned to the U.S. Ezaldeen felt compelled to take the Sunni path. According to some he initially wanted to start his organization in the state of Pennsylvania but was denied a charter by state officials. As a result, Newark, a Moorish-American stronghold by this time, claimed one of the former AAUAA members, became an attractive alternative for his plans. Newark, NJ became the city where Ezaldeen resided until his death in 1957 and his wife Karema

Karema Ezaldeen at AAUAA. (Courtesy of Wahab Arbubakar.)

until 1995. It is not farfetched to conclude that Ezaldeen chose Newark because of the presence of the Moorish-Americans that he had been familiar with in prior years. In an interview with Malik Arbubakar, an
AAUAA member since childhood, he states:

> I remember when I was a kid, I remember Professor Ezaldeen mentioning to me about the Shriners and Moors, and he acknowledged their existence. I wouldn't say that he was fond of them, because you could tell there was something in the back of his mind, that he had some reservations about them. I remember as a little kid . . . when I would come out on Prince Street, I would see the Moors with their red fezzes on and their tassels. And he, Professor Ezaldeen, would acknowledge them. I would not say that it was a love hate relationship, but I think he acknowledged them with a certain distance.[37]

Ezaldeen's reserved attitude undoubtedly was influenced by his experiences in Egypt and other Muslim nations abroad, and perhaps his prior experiences with the Moorish-American community.

NOTES

1. Heshaam Jaaber, interview by author, Elizabeth, NJ June, 1997.
2. Dennis Walker, *Islam and the Search for African-American Nationhood*, (Atlanta,Georgia: Clarity Press, 2005), 243.
3. Ezaldeen was James Lomax before the name change. Ezaldeen changed his name more than once. He was also known as James Lomax Bey or simply Lomax Bey.
4. This is mentioned in *The Universal Truth*, Volume 2 No 3.
5. Walter Arthur McCray, *The Black Presence in the Bible*, (Chicago: Blacklight Fellowship, 1990), 54.
6. By the time that the AAUAA became active in Newark in 1941, the Moorish American community had already set the stage for the wearing of the red fez. In fact, the wearing of the red fez was common even among many of the Ahmadi Muslims who were very active in New York by this time.
7. Talib, interview by the author, Elizabeth, New Jersey, June 1997.
8. Isa Muhammad. *Who was Noble Drew Ali*, revised edition, (Brooklyn, New York: Ansaru Allah Community, 1988), 45.
9. Walker documents that in 1930 under the name Ali Mohammed Bey, Ezaldeen arrived in Turkey and delivered a petition to Kemal Ataturk on behalf of 28,000 Negroes facing prejudice in America. He requested that his sect be allowed to found a colony in Anatolia, Angora or any other under-populated farming area. Turkish officials were, merely, polite. For J. Edgar Hoover, the attempt to relocate to Turkey was a subversive act, harmful to America's international image. See page 243 in *Islam and the Search for African-American Nationhood*.

10. Michael Nash, "The Son of Thunder," Who Was Minister James 3X Shabazz? Nation of Islam History in Newark, NJ—Part II, *Muslim Journal*, November 1, 2002.

11. Nash, "Son of Thunder."

12. Clement Price, "The Beleaguered City as Promised Land: Blacks in Newark, 1917-1947," *Urban New Jersey Since 1870*, edited by William C. Wright, Trenton NJ 1974, New Jersey Historical Commission.

13. *The Universal Truth*, 14.

14. Sati Majid, a Sudanese national and *alim* (scholar) from Dongola and Drew Ali of the Moorish Science Temple had an encounter sometime in the 1920s. Ahmed I. Abu Shouk, J.O. Hunwick & R.S. O'Fahey in an article titled "A Sudanese Missionary to the United States: Satti Majid, Shaykh Al-Islam in North America', and His encounter with Noble Drew Ali, Prophet of the Moorish Science Temple Movement" published in *Sudanic Africa*, 8, 1997, 137-191 states that "sometime in the late 1920s there was an encounter, direct or indirect we do not know for certain, between two figures from two very traditions of 'Islam'. The article provides a glimpse of African-American Islam's earliest encounter with global Islam." It seems likely that Satti Majid's rejection of Drew Ali's teachings helped to facilitate Ezaldeen's acceptance as a student in Egypt since Ezaldeen by this time had had enough of the heterodox teachings of Islam that was so prevalent among African-Americans. Majid had informed some Sudanese and Egyptian religious authorities about the Moorish movement and its founder. As it seems, Ezaldeen traveled abroad with the intentions of finding out for himself the true teachings of Islam. When he returned to the U.S. in 1936 he apparently made a commitment to share his knowledge about what he had learned.

15. *The General Centre World Young Men Muslims Association (Pamphlet)*, Cairo, United Arab Republic. Atlas Press 11, 13, Souk el Tewfikia, Cairo, page 39.

16. *The General Centre*, 37.

17. *The General Centre*.

18. *The General Centre*, 41.

19. Shahada is the declaration that one must make upon accepting al-Islam into their hearts. The declaration is as follows: I bear witness that there is no God but Allah and I bear witness that Muhammad is his Messenger. It is usually made in the presence of at least two or more witnesses.

20. There are many local stories about this.

21. Mentioned in Mustafa El-Amin's *The Religion of Islam and the Nation of Islam: What is the Difference?*

22. Amir Al-Islam, "Beyond Malcolm: Muslim Leadership of the 21st Century," *The Message*, October 26th 1996.

23. Abdullah Hakim Quick, *Islam and the African in America: The Sunni Experience*, (Mississauga, Ontario Canada: The Islamic Academy of Canada, 1997) Endnote #29.

24. [Addeynu Allahe Universal Arabic Association Inc.?] Our Story Nowhere: Nonesuch Press, 8. This official literature of the organization was shared by Wahab Arbubakar. Ezaldeen probably served as a public school teacher somewhere in the state of Pennsylvania.

25. "[Addeynu Allahe] Our Story."

26. Talib "Interview."

27. *Qur'an* 49:13.

28. The english translation for *Jamaat* is community. This term is commonly used by most Muslim Americans, even those whose native tongue is English.

29. "[Addeynu Allahe] Our Story."

30. "[Addeynu Allahe] Our Story."

31. Malik ArbuBakar, Interview by author, Newark, NJ, 19 October 1997.

32. Heshaam Jaaber, *The Final Chapter. . . . I Buried Malcolm (Haj Malik El-Shabazz),* (Jersey City, NJ.: New Mind Productions, 1992), 64.

33. Jaaber, *The Final Chapter*, 64.

34. The 1968 Report of the National Advisory Commission on Civil Disorders, *The Kerner Report*, (New York:Pantheon Books, 1988), 73.

35. Abdullah Yasin, "A Message to the African American Muslim", *Shahada* 2, No 4, Oct-Dec 1997: 5.

36. Walker, *Islam and the Search for African-American Nationhood*, 244.

37. Malik ArbuBakar, Interview by author, 30 November 1997.

Chapter Six

The Expansion

AFTER EZALDEEN: A GLIMPSE AT BAITUL QURAISH

With the passing of Professor Ezaldeen the AAUAA members stayed together for a few years, but then suffered some internal problems that resulted in a split. Sometime in the early to mid 1960s one of Ezaldeen's students Akeel Karam broke away from the parent organization and established Masjid Deenul-Lah near Clinton Place. Both Deenul-Lah and the AAUAA continued to maintain their allegiance to the Hametic Arab identity and both maintained some distance from the MSTA and the NOI. They were interested in building on the foundation that Ezaldeen had laid in Newark for the institutionalization of Sunni Islam.

Baitul Quraish, another group not previously connected (to any significant degree) to the NOI or MSTA, became an influential Sunni Muslim group in Newark from about 1969 to 1975. Led by the late Kamiel Wadud (also known as Phillip Walker), the organization emerged and established a visible presence in the city. Emphasis was placed on establishing institutions that provided food, clothing and shelter. Wadud and his beloved wife endeavored to establish an economic base for the Muslim community, by selling door to door clothes which were purchased from clothing manufacturers. At the start of this business venture they used their private station wagon for this purpose. Eventually, enough money was raised to purchase a truck that was used to transport more clothes. As the business became lucrative, additional trucks were bought and parked during off-business hours on Bayview Avenue, Newark, where the organization's headquarters was located. After they were successful in purchasing three trucks, it became necessary for them to secure a larger space in a non-residential area to park the trucks. Due to Wadud's keen business sense, he was able to secure for the

Akeel Karam at AAUAA. (Courtesy of Wahab Arbubakar.)

organization a building and a large lot on South 18th Avenue as a step towards institutional development. In addition to having space for a masjid and a school, the newly acquired space had a parking lot that was large enough to hold the nineteen trucks that the organization eventually purchased to run its clothing business.

Unlike Ezaldeen, Wadud did not receive any formal Islamic Education. Described by his wife as a very generous man and exceptional human being, Sheik Kamiel, as he was generally known, was said to have acquired a reputation as a peacemaker in the state of New Jersey as well as a defender of Islam, and of the rights of Muslims. He represented Muslim interests and concerns at many municipal gatherings as well. Not only was his leadership valued by many Muslims at that time, but he was recognized as a respected community leader among Newark officials. Former members of the Baitul Quraish organization remember him as not only having street smarts, but a type of charisma that was applied on several levels. As it seems, most people who came into contact with him trusted his judgment. It has been said that one of his major qualities was his gift for tapping into the strengths of other people, and using these strengths for the benefit of the community. In hindsight, some former members have criticized Wadud for his failure to effectively distribute power and resources amongst the people; however, most agree that the moral lessons and practical experience that they acquired as a result of being active in his Muslim community were positive ones, and remain with them to this day. Amiri Baraka, the widely celebrated poet/activist who had some dealings with him during the 1960s, described Wadud as a kind of street gangster, at one time, who had received the religion of al-Islam and had been transformed.[1]

By the time that this organization was founded in the late 60s, the desire for Muslim community development in the area was in high demand, and as it would seem, Muslim community development was ready to move into its next phase. African American Muslims came from many parts of the country to join the community of Baitul Quraish. For them, Newark in many respects had become the Mecca of the United States of America. Some Muslim families migrated to Newark because of what they had heard about the Muslims in this area. As one member who immigrated to Newark during the late 60s said, "from Detroit Michigan, we learned of this Muslim community in Newark, New Jersey, that housed their own, fed their own and clothed their own, and had their own school and *masjid*, and we were attracted to that."[2]

Although it did not receive the type of attention that the Nation of Islam did, Baitul Quraish seemed to have been an attractive alternative to the Nation of Islam movement that began to make a considerable presence in the city during the early 1960s. As was mentioned, Professor Ezaldeen had already laid the foundation for the practice of Sunni Islam in the area. His contribution made it possible for Newarkers to be exposed to the Sunni (orthodox) path since 1941. It is my belief that members of the African American community became interested in learning about the orthodox teachings of the religion due to the emphasis that such teachings places on the unity of mankind. These African Americans exercised their right to choose another path. The right of an individual to choose is a fundamental value which Islam since its inception in the seventh century supported. Arguably, the orthodox path had an inherent strength in it that could serve as an explanation for why the Greater Newark area is dominated today by Sunni Islam. This is important to mention because Americans are used to the theory that because African Americans, historically, have been the victims of white racism since the 17th century, this reality, very often, has encouraged them to adopt black nationalist philosophies. On the contrary, few have considered the possibility that orthodoxy was also a response to their being victims of white racism. The difference is that their response was a call to the establishment of justice in a racially oppressive and polarized society. The Qur'an is very explicit on how Muslims should deal with injustices of all sorts. It states:

> O You who believe! Be ever ready in your devotion to Allah, bearing witness to the truth in all equity, and never let hatred of others lead you to deviate from justice. Be just, this is closest to righteousness. And remain conscious of Allah: verily, Allah is aware of all that you do.[3]

It should be understood that, like the AAUAA, Baitul Quraish emphasized the need for African American Muslims to identify with the Hametic Arab classification, which clearly shows the influence of Ezaldeen. They felt that it was important for Muslims in their association to know about and understand their lineage as well as their religious heritage. While he was respected among some international Muslim figures, like Ezaldeen, Wadud was careful not to surrender the community's autonomy and integrity to foreign influence. Members of Baitul Quraish also adopted the Hametic Arab classification from the AAUAA. This was essential because it gave them a new identity that suggested a racial connection to the biblical figure, Ham, who is often referred to as the father of the black race. They also felt a spiritual connection to Arabia since southern Arabia, particularly, is often said to be Hamitic in origin. Thus, this organization did not only place emphasis on the learning of Islamic principles and theory, but also heritage. As the famous saying of the Egyptians, "know thy self," has become a sort of liberation call among many African Americans, this nostalgic identification with a Hametic Arab heritage was a response to that call. But, more importantly, to the Muslims in Newark, it was a response to the call of Allah who said in the Qur'an that "I created you (mankind) into nations and tribes so that you will know one another, not that you may despise one another . . . the best of you in the sight of Allah is the one who is most regardful of their duties to their Lord."[4] They also encouraged their members to learn Arabic, especially the Qur'anic Arabic. It was common, especially during Eid celebrations, for believers to practice reading and understanding the Arabic text of the Qur'an.[5] To learn to read and understand the Qur'an in Arabic was a common goal of all members of the community. In addition to implementing Islamic studies, Wadud encouraged and motivated the believers to work hard to establish a strong community base that would serve as a sanctuary for Muslim families, and also serve as a visible example of the power of *iman* (faith in God) to the outside community. With great enthusiasm, the community of Baitul Quraish strove to implement his ideas and turn them into a practical reality, and as a result had a significant impact on the growth and development of Islam in Newark. Although the community suffered some serious economic hardships around 1973, causing many families to branch out on their own, Baitul Quraish was undoubtedly the first among the Sunnis in Newark to take on the challenge of building a community where all members depended on one another for their livelihood.

As the record shows, Baitul Quraish was the first community in the city to open up a *halal* (permissible by Islamic Law) meat market at 1048 Bergen Street in Newark. The building where this business was located no longer exists, but it had a meat market on the first floor and apartments on the second

and third floors. As most people know, Islam has strict dietary laws, pro-
hibiting to its adherents pork, alcohol, and meat not slaughtered according to
what is permissible by Islamic Law. The Sunni Muslims had made a special
effort to consume *halal* meat, but it was often difficult due to the absence of
halal meat stores. Oft-times they found themselves in the situation where they
had to at least consume non-alcoholic and non-pork products even if the
source which these items came from were not strictly prepared according to
the Islamic Law.[6] And although the Qur'an had made it permissible for Muslims to consume the meat of the People of the Book (that of the Jews and
Christians) the Muslim community in Newark, under Wadud's leadership,
took the initiative to develop a halal meat industry so that the Muslim community would not have to depend on others such as the Jewish and Christian
communities to satisfy their dietary needs.

There were many challenges that the community faced, and economics were
among them. When it first started in the late 1960s, the members were renting
an apartment which they had leased at 709 South 26th street. This building no
longer exists either. Quite naturally, as the community grew, the need for expansion became imminent. In a relatively short period of time, within approximately five years, Baitul Quraish was successful in acquiring real estate to
house a school for the children of the community and a *masjid* for the believers in Newark. These institutions were instrumental in educating people about
the orthodox teachings of al-Islam. Members in the community understood that
the establishment of such institutions was a necessary sacrifice for the preser-
vation of an Islamic identity in the city and the Islamic cause. This, the members felt, was their duty as believers in the faith. Similarly, they wanted to continue and build upon the work of Professor Ezaldeen, and bring about a feeling
of independence, respect, and economic stability that was so desperately
needed among African Americans. Although they were not associated with the
Nation of Islam, which should be remembered for its truly great legacy of
championing these causes among African Americans, the fact still remains that
Baitul Quraish sought to accomplish the same objectives of acquiring independence, respect and economic stability, but unlike the Nation it endeavored to do
this without compromising its position on orthodoxy.

Baitul Quraish felt a connection with the international Muslim community
as well. Interestingly enough, this community, while remaining loyal to Dr.
Aminah Beverly McCloud's idea of ummah also seemed to have employed
certain aspects of *asabiya* through its identification with the Hametic Arab
classification. This scholar states:

> *Asabiya* refers to the idea of nation-building among people of the same ethnic-
> ity and with a common history . . . *Ummah*, on the other hand, is a concept that

refers to group affiliation and, in general Arabic usage, the term has been employed to designate a community, a nation, and/or a generation . . . In *Qur'anic*
usage, the term *ummah* refers to the community of believers who struggle in unison to submit their will to the Will of Allah . . . The idea of *ummah* has been cast
as something that is basically opposed to *asabiya*, such that a person or community must decide whether to make its priority the formation of *asabiya* or the
experience of *ummah* . . . African American Muslim communities are largely understood and differentiated by whether they grant priority to nation-building or
to the experience of *ummah* and participation in the world Islamic community.[7]

From its inception, Baitul Quraish was committed to the idea of *ummah* because of its commitment to the principle of *tauhid*, which is central to Islam
and everything Islamic. Interestingly enough, one could argue that it was also
committed to *asabiya* due to its adherence to the Hamitic Arab identity.

Mainstream media, in its efforts to report on the growth of the Islamic influence in America in the twentieth century, did not provide a great deal of
fair coverage on any Muslim community, but this was especially true with the
African American Sunnis. With the help of mainstream media, the Nation of
Islam emerged in the popular imagination of Americans as the model community for the establishment of al-Islam in America. This is true despite the
fact that Sunni communities among African Americans have existed in the
United States since the early 1930s when many of them became disenchanted
with the missionary activities of the Indian Ahmadiyyah Movement. A case
in point is the First Cleveland Mosque, founded by Wali Akram. "Akram, an
African American covert to Islam in St. Louis in 1925, is reported to have
founded the First Cleveland Mosque in 1932, which is now the oldest con-
tinuously running [Sunni] Muslim institution in the United States."[8] Historically, from a national stand point the Nation of Islam also emerged around
1932. But, within the context of Newark history, the Sunni religious institutions among African Americans predate the establishment of Nation of Islam
temples by eighteen to twenty years. More than the NOI, arguably, the Sunni
community have over the course of its development, had to acquire its successes without the help of the mainstream media. Similarly, even "most
scholars writing about Islam in the African American communities have fo-
cused their efforts on the examination of the teachings of the Nation of Islam,"[9] states McCloud. She continues by stating,

in particular, their interest seems to have centered on a critique of the Nation's
philosophy concerning the origin of the Caucasian race, a preoccupation of
non-Muslim as well as Muslim writers. This obsession with the teachings about
race has led to two major lacunae in our understanding of the dynamics of Islam in society. First, we have relatively little informed data about the growth

and development of an equally large Islamic population outside the Nation of Islam, that of the Sunni African Americans who have been active in the major urban areas of the United States since the first quarter of this century.[10]

Some Muslims have charged that the media intentionally tried to push the Nation of Islam into the light of the American public in order to subvert the programs of the Sunni community. Historians, similarly, have done little to record the efforts of Muslims who have tried to meet their civic duties as an American citizen. A case in point is the late Otis King, an observant Muslim of mixed heritage (African-American and European) who ran on the democratic ticket for mayor of Newark in the 1960s. King was not affiliated with the NOI. Further, a few have charged that there was a government conspiracy to hide Muslim-American achievements and contain Islamic thought and to keep the American people confused about the true peaceful nature of Islam and its potential for unifying people across racial and ethnic lines. Be that as it may, our purpose in acknowledging the fact that the Sunnis among African Americans were active observers of key pillars of the Islamic faith at least thirty-four years before the NOI is not intended to devalue or diminish any of the positive contributions to Newark or American society made by the Nation of Islam. The intent here is simply to accurately outline the sequence of events as a matter of historical record.

Most Sunnis believe that al-Islam is the universal religion that cuts across racial boundaries. As a consequence, they have insisted that while the Nation of Islam's philosophy had some admirable qualities in the areas of economic and social philosophy, its theological and spiritual base was way off center due to its position on race, which contradicted the concept of *tauhid*. While the Sunni community was foremost in projecting a more accurate view of Islam relative to its position on race, it was less successful than the Nation of Islam in reaching its long-term economic goals and making a political impact. This reality is beginning to shift. The reasons, though, for the developmental variations, are multifaceted. However, Dr. Akbar Muhammad perhaps said it best when he stated that "American Muslims are a disparate group of people searching for an acceptable *modus vivendi* in a world of appealing materialism, customs, ideals, and ideologies which offend their sensibilities and conflict with the traditions of their faith."[11] No doubt, Newark is a case in point. In Greater Newark, Muslims have not come to a consensus on how to interpret doctrine so as to implement a cohesive Islamic community life effectively. This compounded with the societal pressures of poverty, urban life, media insensitivity, and adjustment to a new way of viewing the world and their role in it, has made it difficult for them to establish the type of unity that is necessary for a long-term community development program. Further distractions are caused by the demands for relief from the debilitating effects of the drug culture, gang violence, health concerns, social services and the lack of sufficient services for young African American males who have been incarcerated compared to white males at a disproportionate percentage. In spite of these difficulties, African American Muslims in the Greater Newark area are pioneers. As the record shows, Baitul Quraish during the 1970s was successful in spearheading a solid effort to establish a community-base where members depended upon one another for their livelihood. The men and women in this community understood the magnitude of their circumstances, which encouraged them even more to work towards communal living.

Historically, Baitul Quraish was perhaps the first to establish a visible model for Muslim community development in Newark. They had many successes and made many mistakes in the process of building its community, which resulted in some failures. Many of the members shared the same living quarters, and thus had to learn to depend upon one another for their livelihood. This, essentially, is the meaning of community. Members lived a very modest life and depended much upon an intricate barter system for their survival. The members were mostly interested in furthering their knowledge about al-Islam. The development of a micro-Muslim economy was encouraged and supported by members as well as by a high distressed non-Muslim community, which became a major market for Baitul-Quraish's clothing business during the 1970s. The Amir of the community Kamiel Wadud allotted as little as sixty or seventy dollars a week on an average, to each household (approximately 27 families), which was used to buy food, clothing, to do laundry, and to take care of other necessities. Sometimes finances would get extremely tight, and in extreme cases some families would have to make ends meet on as little as $15.00 a week. A former member stated the following:

> We were given subsidies which I didn't like. Subsidies were the amount of money that was distributed per family. It was two families in each household. We rotated cooking and cleaning, and each family would get a subsidy every other week. One family would get a subsidy one week, and the other family the next week, and it was never enough. So one of the things I learned in Baitul Quraish was that you should never allow anyone to control your food, clothing and shelter—your basic necessities.[12]

The adult male members found it lucrative to purchase clothes from clothing manufacturers in New York and Elizabeth and then sell them at retail prices. This idea started out small and then evolved into a major enterprise that became the economic life-source of the community. According to one version of the story, "it all started when a brother from Elizabeth who was a part of the AAUAA would go to clothing outlets in Elizabeth, New Jersey and buy a dozen shirts and dresses so that he could sell them in the streets and make a little money and donate it to the masjid." The enterprise mushroomed when the Muslims, under Sheik Kamiel's direction, went to a public auction in Newark during the early 1970s and bought some old PSE&G cars. They fixed up the cars, loaded them up with clothes, and went around the streets of Newark, selling them to people in need of these items. In this sense, they were able to provide a service to the Newark community at-large, and at the same time support the economic goals of the Baitul Quraish community. Within a short period of time, Baitul Quraish eventually acquired enough money to purchase some old mail trucks, which made it possible for the members to transport larger quantities of clothes. These trucks were painted yellow to camouflage the old paint. By 1973, the community reportedly had acquired sixteen trucks of which seven were operable and out on the streets of Newark on any given day. The members use to ride up and down the streets shouting, "dress-van, dress-van", and the people became accustomed to coming out to buy clothes at affordable prices. One former member stated that "when the housing projects were erected on Howard Street, we used to go over there and on any given day, we would average about $400 per truck." "Around the first of each month, we would average about $1200 per truck a day." The merchandise consisted of men's and women's clothes, children's clothes and children's shoes. They mainly carried, however, ladies and little girl's clothes. And due to the connections that Sheik Kamiel had, the merchants were ofttimes able to by-pass the middle man and negotiate directly with the manufacturers.

A typical day for those who worked on the trucks entailed handling daily duties around the community, such as religious instruction and settling family issues. At about four or five o'clock in the afternoon, the trucks would start rolling out to sell clothes. In most cases, they would stay out to about two o'-clock in the morning, even though they had to be up for the Fajr (Early Morning Prayer) in most cases at about five a.m. During this period, the clothing business did very well.

Although Baitul Quraish initiated the halal meat business in Newark, it proved to be difficult to maintain. Like other industries, the halal meat industry was affected by the negative trends of the world economy during the 1970s. A case in point is the international oil embargo of 1972. During this time, U.S. policy makers were concerned about the leverage that Middle Eastern countries had attained through its control of oil prices in the global arena. Since the U.S. was largely dependent upon Middle Eastern oil, it became anathema for Americans (Muslim or non-Muslim) to outwardly express any sensitivity to the Islamic world. Quite naturally, this climate did not serve the interest of Muslim Americans who were often labeled as subversives along with black revolutionaries of the 1960s era. Yet, the oil embargo had an indirect impact on the micro-economy of the Muslims in Newark at that time. A former member said:

> To show you the impact that the oil embargo had on us, we were paying 33 cents a pound for a steer, and these steers would weigh from 1500 to 2000 pounds. But, after the oil embargo, it went from 33 cents to 1.75 cents a pound. It sort of stifled us. Also, gas prices were 59 cents a gallon. But after the oil embargo, it went up to 99 cents a gallon. We had seven trucks going out every day; the increase in the price of gas contributed to the difficulty.

This testimony reveals the extent to which national and international factors contributed to the domestic problems of the Newark Muslim community. The establishment of the halal meat industry was a priority of the Sunnis. Although the NOI forbade its members from consuming pork which is a requirement of the Islamic Law, the establishment of the halal meat industry in the NOI Newark community developed much later. For all Muslims, to eat halal meat meant more than just not to eat pork, but rather to consume meat that was slaughtered according to the Islamic Law. As is evident, orthodoxy relative to the consumption of food was something that was valued greatly. Because the Sunnis had internalized the meanings of the ayats (Quranic verses) relative to the consumption of food, perhaps they, out of conviction, could not put off until later the need to establish the halal meat industry.

As students of Muslim-American history study the trends and developments in the evolution of the Muslim American community, it is essential to differentiate between the teachings of the various Sunni groups among African Americans who were not influenced by the Nation of Islam versus the teachings of those who accepted the leadership of Imam W.D. Muhammad upon his father's death. Their teachings converge and diverge on many points. Lack of communication between them in my judgment, are at the root of many of the problems that Muslim Americans face. Further, although Sunni Muslims in the area, as a whole, share similar views, there are important differences as a result of different historical circumstances that have played a major role in how decisions were made in the interest of the Muslim community.[13]

Baitul Quraish developed relationships with Muslims from overseas to assist with learning the religion and the Arabic language. Muslim brothers from foreign countries would send cases of reading materials that were in Arabic as a contribution to the school. Members used to pick these materials up from JFK airport and transport them to the school to be used for study of the Arabic language and Islam. Sometimes confusion would surface within the Muslim community as a result of the way Islam was taught. The question of what is a true Muslim versus what is an Arab and how these questions related to the experience and identity of African Americans would sometimes cause tension. This sentiment is captured in the testimony of one former member who stated:

> In my college experience, this college professor talked to me about the way that they practiced Islam in Africa and all of the cultural nuances that they had there. She said, they never tried to be Arabs, but in this country they tried to make us Arabs. They tried to make us do all of the things that Arabs did.[14]

In 1975 the community went into decline. It experienced its worst economic hardship around 1976. Because it became increasingly difficult to provide for their families, many of the members left the community to secure gainful employment. Some took advantage of some of the gains made for African Americans during the 70s in the areas of education, jobs, and political appointments, gains that were made largely as a result of the Civil Rights Struggle and the Black Power Movement. Kenneth Gibson, the first black mayor in the city of Newark, took office in 1970. His success was significantly helped by the contributions of Amiri Baraka, who was the leader of the Black Arts Movement in Newark at that time. State sponsored programs sprung up such as the Educational Opportunity Fund (EOF), an affirmative action program started in the late 60s. This program made it possible for disadvantaged minorities, especially African Americans, to attend New Jersey colleges and receive monetary and academic support services with government assistance. The criterion was that an applicant had to demonstrate that he/she had the potential, and the willingness to work hard to achieve success in college. Applicants had to also show that they resided in a high distress area that had a tradition of historical poverty. Newark became one of those designated cities. Thus, many African Americans and young Muslims among them began to explore and take advantage of these options.

Nevertheless, the former members of Baitul Quraish experienced what it was truly like to live in a Muslim community, where people depended upon one another for their very livelihood. This made it possible for them to see and experience many things about community development that many Muslims in the area today can not claim. Of course, there were some pleasant experiences and some not so pleasant ones. Interestingly, it was not uncommon for some members to observe a new life coming into the world, because almost all of the children born in the community were delivered by people in the community, in most cases, Sheik Kamil and his wife. In the words of one former member:

We delivered our children. We saw death in the community we saw all things that is out here, and I'm saying this because it was a learning experience. We saw homosexuality, we saw child molestation. We saw all of that and we dealt with it. We saw the fornicators and the drug abusers, and we dealt with those things in our community as well, and as a result, it helped us grow and it strengthened us. To this day, any brother who was in Baitul Quraish, it's like brother, you were there.[15]

The Sunni communities, perhaps more than the NOI, have been criticized for being sympathetic to the problems of Muslims in other parts of the world. The Nation of Islam has endured similar criticisms, although it is generally known for speaking out more forcefully on the issues relative to blacks on the African continent, in America and throughout the rest of the African Diaspora. Because of this, the Nation of Islam has acquired a certain respect from many among the masses of black people. Nevertheless, this political posturing and watchdog role that the NOI has played have sometimes been perceived as being in conflict with the global political interest of the United States. The lay-man, as a result of government and media insensitivity on these matters, over the years, has been manipulated to be suspicious about exactly where Muslim American's loyalties lie. What many American literary and political critics have suggested is that Muslim political attitudes have been shaped in large part by the social, political and economic conditions of which they have had to cope. Racism and greed by corporation owners is at the root of this national and international menace. This analysis goes beyond pointing a finger at the white power structure or subscribing to the conspiracy theory. In fact, in spite of centuries of white injustice, Muslim Americans have taken a pro-active, self-help and nonviolent approach to addressing the injustices of the oppressed. There has been a constant call for Muslim community development as opposed to thoughts of overthrowing of the United States government. Historically, the various Muslim communities in America have not entertained the idea, nor have any respected leader among them ever been accused or proven guilty of such conspiracies, despite the fact that the *Declaration of Independence* that was drafted by America's founding forefathers as a protest against the British, stated that citizens were within their rights to replace a corrupt and oppressive government. On the contrary, Muslims have approached Muslim community development from the premise that change begins from the inside out. The approach was always that believers must first clean up their own house. For African Americans who would become attracted to any one of the various Islamically-oriented groups, justice consisted of having the freedom to practice the religion, learn about their cultural heritage, and to invite others to join in the establishment of a community that placed emphasis on the need to develop a strong moral as well as economic, and political foundation. For them, Islam would offer the best opportunity to build this three-part foundation. Although Baitul Quraish did not enjoy long-term success, its legacy has some merits, as some have expressed, that ought to be considered by future generations—namely, the desire to become connected politically with the various sectors of civil society, the desire to establish a strong economic base for the development of education and religious institutions as well as social service agencies.

Also worthy of mention is that Baitul Quraish and another small but significant organization by the name of Baitul Khaliq (Newark Community Masjid) tried to influence the culture of African Americans. Abdallah Yasin, the Amir of the Baitul Khaliq community, states, "separate and apart, both organizations attempted and succeeded in the development of tribal naming systems within their respective community/congregation . . . There were several major families within each organization . . . When a person accepted/returned to Islam they could choose to become affiliated with the family of the person through whom they came into the organization. As Yasin states in a book he wrote, *Islamizing America*, "this was an honest attempt by early leadership to put into use [or restore] the displaced family spirit, which everyone needs; the family spirit which in most cases became displaced upon one's acceptance of Islam."[16] This was confirmed by a former member of Baitul Quraish who migrated to the Newark area from Detroit in the late 60s. He states:

> Yes, we had tribal leaders. The community was broken up into tribes—the Waduds, the Ismails and the Ishaacs. Most of the Waduds lived on Bayview Avenue. Most of the Ismails lived at 538 16 St. Sheik Kamil Wadud was the head . . . When I came from Detroit my name was Khalid Abdul Jabbar and I took on the name Ismail to be a part of the Ismail tribe. My name is Khalid Abdul Jabbar Ismail. There was also the Waduds. Malik was the tribal leader of the Waduds. Dawud was the tribal leader of the Ismails and brother Yasin was the tribal leader of the Issacs. The Ishaacs was the smallest tribe in the whole community. The Ismails I think was the largest.[17]

One has to consider what life was like in that time and era. The Muslim elders provide many vivid memories. Ahmed Batemon, a United States veteran and also a Rutgers University graduate stated:

> One day I was coming down 18th Avenue after doing my shopping. I saw the Shaykh and Abdul Muhmi and some of the brothers from Baitul Quraish who was at that time at 476 18th Ave, and they were taking chickens out of a truck or van. They were like passing them along in a chain into the store, and I swear it was the most beautiful thing I had saw in a long time. They were all happy you know and they were laughing and it reminded me of Walt Whitman, a poem

by Whitman about a man and his sons and how happy they were, how full of life and strength you know. When I saw that it just intrigued me.[18]

Batemon expressed his admiration and respect for the efforts made by the Baitul Quraish community. He states:

Baitul Quraish was an Islamic community. The members were trying to establish a community. They wanted to make a place, a niche in the midst of all of this madness, where people could practice Islam, you know what I mean . . . where Islam would be a viable force and it could invite by example. This is what Islam is all about. They wanted to show people that it was possible to live an Islamic life in America. They taught that you could be clean, and you could be sober and chaste, and that you could have a whole family structure.[19]

Although he was not affiliated with the Nation of Islam, Batemon admired and respected certain aspects of the organization. In response to the question, "is it accurate to say that most of the influence of Islam came through the Nation of Islam, even though the Nation was not practicing the Sunnah, he stated the following:

I realized through my own trials and tribulations that the only way that a person can make it being black, you understand, is to have a structured life. You can't just be here. Under any other circumstances and under any other skin, it might be possible to just float around and be free, you see; and to have a structure around you, protected. But it is only we, us (black people), we have to make a structure, and it has to be an individual effort on the part of each of us. And if with the structure that we make, we can hook up with something greater, and make that greater, then all well and good. But without a structure we will not survive. Now the Nation regardless of whether you agreed with it or not, started with a structure.[20]

Heshaam Jaaber was also among the first who was involved in Islamic work in the Greater Newark area. Like Wahab Arbubakar, Musa Hamad and others not mentioned here, he received his Islamic education directly under Professor Ezaldeen. Jaaber has stated that what he learned through the Addeynu Allahe Universal Arabic Association equipped him with the knowledge to educate Americans about Islam. He too has vivid memories of the struggle of Sunni Muslim pioneers in the Greater Newark area. He states:

I came to Elizabeth, New Jersey around 1949, right on Pennsylvania Avenue. It wasn't until 1955 that I really began to get into the dawah. It was this year that I got out of the military and came back here, and I met a brother from the Addeynu Allahe Universal Arabic Association Inc. called Abdullah Majied and then he introduced me to Wahab Arbubakar. The organization met on Prince Street in Newark. We use to meet in a little place upstairs. Then we moved down to Hawthorne Avenue. I believe I was among the first who called themselves Hamites to do the first khutbah (Islamic sermon) in Newark. I made hajj the first time in 1962. I buried Malcolm in 1965. I traveled from here across the country before that, and I was in at one time Hampton Institute. I gave twenty students their shahada at one time. I acquired my Islamic knowledge through the Addeynu Allahe Universal Arabic Association. Also, I have a background in religion and theology because in my family I have black Jews; I have Moors; and I have Christians. Most of the Christians were Ethiopian orthodox.[21]

Those who are familiar with the issues between the proponents of the Sunni and the black-nationalist paths are now beginning to understand the arguments on both sides of the equation. Those who were introduced to Islam through the Nation of Islam followed the black nationalist path and those who were introduced to the faith through influences such as the Ahmadiyyah movement tended to develop a non-racial, multicultural outlook, states Richard Brent Turner in his book, *Islam in the African American Experience*.

In the case of the Addeynu Allahe Universal Arabic Association, which considered it self to be Sunni, the interesting thing is that its approach was both nationalistic and multicultural. The founder and leader of this organization, Muhammad Ezaldeen, an African American who became recognized as a Muslim scholar, dealt with the question of black identity by linking his followers to Ham of the Old Testament. What we know of Ezaldeen's background suggest that in addition to his experiences in Muslim countries, he had a great deal of exposure to people and institutions that would help formulate and crystallize his ideas about black identity. It is likely that his experience in Egypt, the land of the Pharoahs, undoubtedly played a role in adopting and appropriating the term Hametic to American blacks. Many believe that he was encouraged by some Turkish people to go to Egypt in search of knowledge pertaining to black identity. As to whether this advice was given to him in the U.S. or in Turkey itself when he visited there is not known. This is important to mention because some researchers have spoken of a Turkish community that had a place of prayer and an Imam that existed in Newark in the 1920s. Perhaps Ezaldeen crossed paths with some of them. Be that as it may, as we now know, the members of the AAUAA were proud to call themselves Hametics or Hamites. The organization's dawah approach was multicultural in the sense that it did not isolate Hametics by claiming that God favored them exclusively because of their nation or tribe. This approach was similar to that of the Ahmadiyyah movement. However, unlike the Ahmadiyyah movement, which taught its members about the principles of the religion and reframed from teaching separate histories, the AAUAA's Hametic Arab identity gave African Americans an identity that linked them to Ham, a popular ancient black figure, and a non-Western outlook. Also, Hametics, like all Muslims, were encouraged to protect and defend Saudi Arabia's right of sovereignty. It was their belief that the original Arabs from which Hametics descended were of dark hue. They all believed like the 14th century Afro-Arab scholar, Ibn Khaldun,[22] who was revered by many Western scholars and wrote the first introduction to a modern history, that faith was and still is the highest form of identification that a person can belong to, and they believed in the concept of *tauhid*. The historical and symbolic significance of Saudi Arabia to them was that it represented that perspective. This identity, though arguably complex and unfamiliar to most Westerners made it possible for Hametics to cope with the dehumanizing and harsh reality of white supremacy without severing the ties between them and Africa. It also put them in a frame of mind that allowed them to challenge the usefulness of the Western paradigm. The stated aims and objectives of the AAUAA at its founding was the following:

(a) To teach Eastern Culture; to build and maintain a National Institution; to educate and rescue every Hametic-Arab and to bring him back to the highest type of civilization, where he once was; to promote love and good will at home and abroad and to thereby maintain the integrity and sovereignty of Arabia; to disseminate the ancient Arabic and Eastern culture among its members; to correct abuses, relieve oppression and carve for ourselves and our posterity a destiny comparable with our idea of perfect manhood and Allah's purpose in creating us: that we may now save ourselves from the curse of our Creator. (b) to promote and pursue happiness, for it is the goal of human life and endeavor. (c) to usher in the teaching and practice of the One God, Allah, who has no relations, sons or daughters. (d) to promote friendly interest among its members; to develop a fraternal spirit among men, and to inculcate in its members the desire to render voluntary aid and assistance to one another at all times.[23]

For these pioneers, it was a challenge for them to identify with their faith in public settings. During the 1950s white Americans, as well as many African Americans who knew little of Islam, seldom empathized with the feelings of alienation that many young Muslims had growing up. Muslim adults, who in most respects depended on the public school system for their child's education, found it difficult to comfort their young. Even among black people, the Islamic faith for the most part was not acknowledged in the public school system. Malik Arbubakar stated that when he was a child growing up, attending Newark public schools, he received just as much ridicule and curiosity from blacks as he did from whites. "I received quite a bit of ridicule

*Wahab Arbubakar in red fez hat with son, Malik Arbubakar
and Malik's sister, Zaniah, of the AAUAA, 1955, (Courtesy
of Wahab Arbubakar)*

due to my Islamic faith, which is why I refrained from using my Muslim name until I got in high school," he stated. "In high school, however, I insisted upon using my Muslim name."[24]

> From 1953 until 1960, I went to Morton Street School. And from 1960 to 1962 I attended Madison and then West Side High School. It wasn't until near the end of my high school days around 64, 65 that the Muslims on South Orange Ave. had now broken Muslims into the light of the American public. So the point here is that there were kids at West Side who said, oh, okay that's different but had become somewhat familiar with Islam. But in the 50s and what not, to be Muslim in the public schools was like taboo. Europeans looked upon you as a little funny, and they questioned you as to why you would want to go that route. Even my cousin, my best friend at the time, could not understand some of the choices I made connected with my faith.[25]

When Professor Ezaldeen died in 1957 there was a split into at least two factions and the membership went into different directions. In the recollection of Malik Arbubakar, it stayed quiet for a number of years. You really didn't hear much about Al-Islam until the early 1960s, when Elijah Muhammad came out with his *Muhammad Speaks*, he states.

This is what brought the name of Islam and Muslim back onto the forefront. On the flip side, the Sunni Muslims were doing things but quietly . . . they were never rabble-rousers. The Temple #25 on South Orange Avenue started to recruit heavily, and they are the ones who, no matter how you look at it, positive or negative, they brought a lot of attention to the word Muslim in the Newark area. Malcolm X brought a lot of light to Al-Islam in the Newark area. Even though we did not necessarily believe in some of Malcolm's and Elijah's teachings, we understood what they were trying to accomplish.[26]

The 1960s was a very tumultuous time for the country, especially in urban America. In Newark the social problems were worsening, especially in areas where blacks were highly concentrated. Otto Kerner stated in a federal report that the "typical ghetto cycle of high unemployment, family breakup, and crime was present."[27] As one observer put it, Newark blew up in the summer of 1967. People were frustrated, tired, afraid and uncertain of what the future might bring. As a result of these fears, a rebellion occurred and people, largely the urban poor, took to the streets as a form of protest against the injustices of government, property owners, and police brutality. It was called the "long hot summer" because of the terrible riots, looting, and burning that devastated the black sections of so many of America's cities. The problem became so urgent that President Lyndon B. Johnson saw the need to appoint a special commission chaired by Illinois governor, Otto Kerner, to study the cause of these disturbances. "The Commission pointed to the continued polarization of American society, the persistence of white racism, and other factors, and argued that only a compassionate, massive, and sustained government effort could reverse the overall trend toward a racially divided, separate and unequal society."[28] This report was made back in 1968. Since then, the gains made by African Americans in the 60s and 70s had slipped away in the 80s. Twenty years later, Vermont Rochester stated the following in the 1988 edition of the Kerner Report:

> The urban ghetto is, if anything, more populous, confining, and poverty-ridden than in 1968. Despite the rise of a small and tenuous black "middle class," the overall economic position of blacks is little improved. Black median family income, which rose to 61.5 percent of the white median in 1975, had dropped back to 57.5 percent by 1985, almost no gain since the 1950s. Black unemployment continues to measure approximately twice that of whites.[29]

Those who fought courageously for civil rights felt especially slighted by these setbacks. Their reasoning was that they fought so hard to get legislation passed so that blacks could live as equals among white Americans.

The approach of the Muslims of Newark for achieving equality was much different in its methodology. Whether one was a part of the Nation of Islam or a member of a Sunni community, the strategy for achieving social equality and material wealth was to embrace the philosophy of doing for self. As the record shows, the Nation of Islam was by far the most successful in this department. For them, the way to achieve social equality and material wealth was to establish a power base made up of skilled black laborers who would toil for the Nation and those who had what was described at that time as a global black and moral consciousness. The Nation's approach was much like that which was advocated by the Tuskegeean, Booker T. Washington in the latter part of the nineteenth century. Unlike his contemporary, W.E.B. DuBois, Washington believed that agitation and fighting for equal rights was not the best way to achieve freedom, justice and equality for African Americans, and he suggested a strong work ethic coupled with an emphasis on establishing an economic power-base. It should be clearly understood that although DuBois and Washington did not see eye to eye on how to achieve black progress, their goals were essentially the same.

I refer to this classic 20th century African American debate to challenge the next generation of historians (Muslim and non-Muslim) to consider the contribution of Muslim leaders, including Elijah Muhammad and later his son and successor, Imam Warithideen Mohammad as representative of another point of view on how to achieve freedom, justice and equality for African Americans. Far too often, Muslim leaders have been examined and viewed from the periphery of the Civil Rights Movement, almost as if there has been no contribution at all. However, the extent to which Muslim personalities and organizations have influenced this country and the lives of people, lends credibility to the idea that Islam has been a positive force for social change in America. The main idea espoused by the Muslim organizations was to do-for-self, an approach that was very similar to that of Booker T. Washington's. Ahmed Burhani, a former secretary of the Newark chapter of the Nation of Islam in the 1960s stated the following in reference to the organization:

> Even though the Muslims at that time were not allowed to engage in the Civil Rights Struggle, there was an affinity that the Muslims, even at that time, had for the people who were involved in that particular struggle. Of course, the line of the Organization (NOI) at that time was that we should not be begging the white man for things that we could and should do for ourselves. That was the general by-law of the Organization at that particular time. But I think the disagreement was one of methodology as opposed to it being what blacks should have, and what they should not have.[30]

One should not misconstrue these statements to mean that members of the Nation of Islam or the Sunni communities were not in favor of getting legislation passed that benefited African Americans, or all Americans for that matter. On the contrary, it is important that one understand these views in historical context. Historically, and as recent as 20th century history, African Americans have been excluded from governmental support and protection. In fact, even when gains were made by them, there was nothing to rescue and preserve them when white backlash unleashed on the African American community as a result of these gains. The Ku Klux Klan and like-minded groups were very vocal in articulating their fears that African Americans and other minority groups were trying to destroy what they believed to be white culture. These groups were terrorist organizations that often used violence and politics to spread their hate philosophy. It should never be forgotten that the NOI philosophy was only a response or a reaction to their white supremacist doctrines that had taken root in the higher echelons of politics and as a result curtailed the possibility of establishing an American society based on true democracy. Indeed, it was this climate that produced the Nation of Islam. As history attests, in the mid nineteen-seventies the Nation of Islam made a transition to a more orthodox approach. The organization faced many challenges as a result of the transition. The sign of the times was that change was imminent.

THE COUNCIL OF THE BROTHERS: SYMPATHIZERS OF THE NATION OF ISLAM

Said to be the prelude to the Nation of Islam in the city of Newark, the Council of the Brothers was an organization that started in the early 1950s. It consisted of about 20 middle aged men who endeavored to elevate the African American community socially and politically. Among the founders were Franky Shabazz, Norman Gaskins, Yusef Shakoor and Hasan Kareem.[31] Hasan Kareem, the leader and founding member, was said to have been at one point a student of Ezaldeen's. The members of the Council more or less served as a fraternal group that depended a great deal upon one another for emotional, spiritual and economic support. Although most were influenced by Elijah Muhammad's teachings, there were some who had regular contact with Professor Ezaldeen's community in the Prince Street area; they would visit him and the Sunni Muslims at his Prince Street address from time to time. In fact, Shakoor states that members of the Council of the Brothers used to sit down regularly with Professor Ezaldeen when he was teaching Islam on Prince Street. Shakoor stated: "I used to go by and sit with him and listen to him, because he was learned."[32]

Yet, the Council, separate and distinct, was a close-knit community that made an effort to provide the basic necessities of life to all of its members. Shakoor stated:

> The Council of the Brothers was brothers. We didn't sleep with each other's girl-friends or wives. We didn't do any of these dirty things to our brothers, rather, we helped our brothers. All the brothers that you may run into—and there are still a few around—they will tell you that we always provided for each other.[33]

Interestingly, according to Shakoor, even though they had not acquired their first Temple until the early 1960s, the Council of the Brothers was the only group in the history of the Nation of Islam that was awarded a Temple number by Elijah Muhammad in person.[34] Elijah was said to have come to Newark in 1958 to honor this group because of its dedication to and success in carrying out the program of the Nation of Islam. A couple of years or more after his visit, the building on South Orange Avenue was purchased and converted to a Temple, and James Shabazz out of Baltimore, Maryland was appointed by Elijah as the first NOI Minister in Newark, New Jersey.[35] Thus, the prelude to the Nation of Islam was the Council of the Brothers. Over time members of the Council became recognized for their community-service work in the African American community. Although, initially, they were not recognized by Elijah, eventually they became known for their work in the city of Newark. Norman Gaskins was particularly important in attracting media attention.

NATION OF ISLAM UNDER MINISTER JAMES 3X SHABAZZ

> That man put the fear of God in me. He said boy, when you get out there and you are not around me, you are going to meet everything and anything. But remember, God (Allah) is always watching you. Always try to make your good outweigh your bad.[36]

> James Ibn Shabazz

The above statement was made by Imam James Ibn Shabazz in reference to his father, the late Minister James 3X Shabazz. The late Minister James 3X Shabazz who was nicknamed by the Honorable Elijah Muhammad, the "Son of Thunder," because of his fiery speeches, was the first official leader of the Newark chapter of the Nation of Islam. The late Imam Armiya Numan described Shabazz as one who had a lot of fire in his preaching of the good news. The NOI community grew tremendously under his tutelage. Neverthe-

less, controversy has surrounded this figure whose legacy is somewhat unde-
fined and skewed. For certain, his death in 1973 was tragic and left a deep
wound in the Newark chapter.

His death has in many ways affected the collective consciousness of the
people who frequented the largest and most popular Nation of Islam Temple
and its subsidiaries in Northern, New Jersey. As to how and why is difficult
to say. However, what can be said with certainty is that the after effect is in-
dicative of a dichotomous relationship between those who admired and valued his style of leadership on the one hand, and those who questioned it on
the other. Yet, the community he left behind in Newark, as a whole, remains
loyal to his person and spirit as he is remembered and celebrated by many as
being another one of Elijah's fine and loyal students. An effort to build a
school in the late Minister's name, in an attempt to rescue his image and that
of the former NOI community from media insensitivity, has been launched by
some who claim to have been positively impacted by Shabazz and knew first
hand of his good works.[37]

It was under Shabazz that the NOI established the University of Islam, a
private school that accommodated grades kindergarten to twelve at one point.
Such schools were established in addition to several businesses that reflected
the Muslim drive towards independence and economic empowerment. It was

Muhammad's Mosque No. 25 in the early 1960s. (Courtesy of Dr. Abdul Salaam.)

not uncommon to see a number of Steak-n-Take restaurants on some of the major streets such as South Orange Avenue and Springfield Avenue. *The Star-Ledger* states:

> In different parts of Newark, especially those areas which were known for solid white businesses before the 1967 riots, Muslims have followed Elijah Muhammad's teachings by opening businesses. A four to five block strip on South Orange Avenue is replete with Muslim restaurants, cleaning establishments and small shops. Chancellor Avenue, Springfield Avenue and other main streets in the South and Central wards have thriving Muslim businesses.[38]

The Newark community also distributed the *Muhammad Speaks* newspaper.

Like the organization's national spokesman at the time, Malcolm X, James 3X Shabazz had a reputation for being a bold and courageous man, somewhat of a shaker and mover. During his tenure he presided over several temples in New Jersey and was the head minister for the northern New Jersey region. His temples were in Newark, Jersey City, Paterson, Plainfield, Elizabeth, Asbury Park, New Brunswick and Atlantic City. Rather than having a minister from those areas conduct the religious services, Shabazz would rotate his Newark assistants. While some found no fault with this approach, some saw this management style as ineffective and felt that it put a strain on the proper functioning of the organization. The New Brunswick arm eventually broke away from Shabazz in the early 1970s and joined the efforts of Minister Louis Farrakhan who was responsible primarily for New York at the time.

Malcolm X was said to have been a personal friend of Minister James 3X Shabazz. On occasion, they would attend meetings and rallies together to promote the program of the Nation of Islam. When Malcolm X was assassinated in 1965 at Harlem New York's Audubon Theatre, Newark because of its popularity and close proximity to New York was at the center of the controversy. Some writers have alluded to the notion that affiliates of the Newark temple at that time played a role in creating the climate that encouraged the assassination or made it possible for it to occur. The other well known factor is the role the intelligence community played in instigating the death of Minister Malcolm. It is no secret that the FBI, through its COINTELPRO (Counter Intelligence Program) kept Malcolm, the NOI, and other black and grassroots organizations under close surveillance.[39] Although Minister James 3X Shabazz was not charged or found guilty of being involved in the alleged conspiracy, like most of the NOI Ministers at that time, his loyalty to Elijah Muhammad when the relationship between him and Malcolm went sour was apparent. Alluding to the peaceful nature and spirit of Islamic brotherhood that had lost its place in the NOI community, the 1965 debacle resulted in "the

Group of Lost Founds in Newark listening to Minister James 3X Shabazz (Courtesy of Dr. Abdul Salaam)

chief Imam [Warith D. Mohammed] saying we were like black devils; and that's what we were," stated Murad Muhammad.[40]

Minister James, too, would meet the same tragic fate eight years later, only two years before Elijah Muhammad would pass away from this life. The *Star-Ledger* reported in 1973 that Minister James was murdered as he pulled in the driveway of his Newark residence.[41] Like Malcolm, although his death was tragic, his spirit and legacy in Newark lives in the hearts of many of those who served under him and benefited from his courageous and productive leadership.

He is most remembered for being a skillful orator and institution builder. Described by Burhani as a strong leader, he was one who believed in and demonstrated the potential of blacks to build their own institutions. This characteristic of the late Minister James has not gone unnoticed by media personalities. Again, the *Star-Ledger* states,

The Muslims' basic tenet that blacks must learn to do things for themselves and not depend on whites, is practiced daily in Newark . . . Between Monday and Friday Muslims in Newark offer an alternative to the city school system. Shortly after 8:30 a.m. school buses stop outside Muhammad Mosque No. 25 on South Orange Avenue, depositing neatly dressed boys and girls on the curb. They line up in twos carrying their book bags and march off to school in Muslim-owned buildings in the area. The classes are segregated, with the boys in some classes and the girls in others. The school was founded six years ago and is fully accredited by the State of New Jersey, offering education through the eighth grade. Called the University of Islam, the school is just one of its kind in U.S. cities.[42]

Though times were difficult without their esteemed leader, the NOI continued to build institutions that addressed the needs and aspirations of urban blacks and Muslims. James Ibn Shabazz stated the following:

> The thing that sustained me was truth and faith in God. When Minister James died, it was a period of reflection for all of us. We felt that God had not brought us this far for nothing. This was a test and a trial for us. We fell back upon our training and teaching and our trust in God. This is what sustained us in those difficult times.

The assassination of strong black leaders, Malik Shabazz and James 3X Shabazz among them, many believed, was a diabolical scheme to disrupt and destroy progress. The goal, according to some, was to kill the spirit of the Muslims in the area during the turbulent 1960s.

NOI WOMEN: SACRIFICING FOR THE NATION

Contrary to the conventional wisdom, many women who joined the Nation of Islam in Newark did so out of personal choice and saw their association with the organization as a means of empowerment and their role as integral to the success of the Muslim community. The discipline that one developed from internalizing and implementing the teachings of Elijah Muhammad contributed to a productive family life that women who joined or courted the organization found attractive.[43] Although NOI women were encouraged—through Shabazz's enthusiasm for and implementation of Elijah's teachings—to take care of the affairs in the home while men worked on the outside, what is often not understood is that women in the context of the NOI set the tone of domestic relations.[44] The main vehicles for socializing the men and women into their respective roles were the Muslim Girls Training (MGT) and the Fruit of Islam Classes (FOI). Many women saw these classes as being very useful and as a source of security for the maintenance of the family. The women in these classes were taught that they were the key to the black man's success, thus minimizing the competition for jobs outside of the home between the man and the woman. The primary responsibility of the women, according to the NOI teachings, was to be a good homemaker for their husband and children.[45]

This would be their contribution to the Nation. The men were expected to toil on the outside in helping to build a nation of productive black people. Because black men would feel the sting of living in a society of having to be dependent, in most cases, on white-owned companies for a job, women were taught and expected to have sensitivity to that reality. Learning to sew, cook, raise children properly and talk to their man in a pleasantly soothing tone — the main function of the MGT classes — was a job in itself. The NOI women had to learn all of this, and made the sacrifice for what they believed to be the success of the future of the Nation. This was the women's contribution to helping break the cycle of dependency that black society had on white society. Cynthia West characterized the impact of Black Muslim women who chose to stay at home in their families as far reaching.[46] "The ramifications of their work she stated was profound, but not often visibly measured; as such, their efforts have largely gone unnoticed, and therefore undervalued."[47] To help us understand the value that the Nation placed on the role of the women, one of the respondents in her study stated the following:

> And I felt like he [the Messenger] was teaching that the black woman is the mother of civilization, and she's your mother. She raised your children. So you have to give her love. So, she can have that love to give to those children, and vice versa. The mother, the woman had to give the man love, so the child would see love in that home, 'cause that's what our children needed. They needed to see that family structure. It was strong. And I thought more than anything, he was trying to build the family structure. Love between the father and the mother and that would make the children have the love.[48]

The family was the foundation of civilization. Therefore stable families, the Nation taught, were necessary for the progress of black people. The well known high moral code of the organization undergirded the stability of most families in Newark. Such things as fornication, adultery, prostitution, pimping, gambling, domestic violence, stealing and other vices were not sanctioned, encouraged or condoned by the official teachings of the NOI. On the contrary, it has been reported that some of the faithful were disciplined or ostracized for their failure to live up to their responsibilities as a member. Family responsibilities were taken very seriously and expectations of each family member within the family unit were very high. This, more often than not, contributed to a stable family. Again, one of the respondents in West's study stated the following:

> Families were pretty stable, because again . . . the brothers had been taught how they were suppose to take care of their families, and they were doin' that. The sisters were bein' taught how she was supposed to take care of that husband, and

they were doin' that. So they fell into line, and you very rarely had any . . . di-
vorces..You didn't see families breaking up. They stayed together, cause it was
that kind of bond thing, and the brothers were very proud of , you know, the fact
that . . . it was unheard of for a single brother to reach a certain age, and not get
married. I mean, you know, everybody was lookin' at 'em a little strange.[49]

None of this should be misconstrued to suggest that NOI men generally
thought that women were not intellectually capable of performing task traditionally characterized as being male roles. Nor did the women think of themselves as intellectually inferior to the men. West stated that when necessary:

Like their male counterparts in the Newark black Community, Black Muslim
women created their own businesses, many of which were run from their homes.
Like nineteenth century women who engaged in domestic money making enterprises, twentieth century Muslim women, too, wished to remain close to their
families. Their work as seamstresses, fish marketers, cooks, and caterers gener-
ated money within the community, supplied needed services, and provided skills
training for Newark community members.[50]

The two-year period between 1973 and 1975 was a very difficult time for
the Muslims of Newark. The Newark community had lost two of its most
powerful and effective leaders in Minister James Shabazz and the Honorable
Elijah Muhammad. The 1973 tragedy was the beginning of a new era in
Newark Muslim history; and when Elijah Muhammad died in 1975, this
marked the beginning of a new era in Muslim American history. The major
media outlets, more often than not, portrayed the events of the period that allegedly were associated with the NOI in very negative terms. It was against
this backdrop that Elijah's son, Wallace D. Muhammad rose to national
prominence.

AFTER ELIJAH: THE INFLUENCE AND
IMPACT OF IMAM W. DEEN MOHAMMED

When the Honorable Elijah Muhammad passed away in 1975, his son, Wallace D. Muhammad, inherited the leadership of the organization. As were
other areas where NOI Temples were established, Newark was surely impacted. Immediately, the Imam, as he came to be known, began to introduce
the Nation of Islam members to new concepts and ideas that were more consistent with the *sunnah* (traditions) of the Prophet Muhammad ibn Abdullah.
From his Chicago headquarters he stressed the importance of the five pillars
of Islam and also placed emphasis on the learning of Arabic. The Imam also

encouraged members to continue their study of black history and to hold on to black pride.

Imam Abdul Kareem Muhammad stated that "one of the key players in helping with the transition from the old teachings to the new was Sheikh Tunis who was instrumental in helping the leaders of the NOI get a better hold on *fiqh*[51] matters and the Sunnah of Prophet Muhammad."[52] But there were a lot of people, Imam Abdul Kareem Muhammad stated, that contributed to educating the community in such things as the proper way of offering salat and implementing the five pillars of Islam into the life of the NOI community.[53] In some sense, the community was struggling to learn the language of the Qur'an, the lessons in the life example of the Prophet Muhammad as they were being acclimated to the new teachings of Imam W. Deen Mohammed at that time. Imam Abdul Kareem stated:

> I think that what really made the transition a little easier for us is that Imam Mohammed, and we have to give him credit, did an excellent job in giving us the knowledge of the Qur'an and the knowledge of the life example of Prophet Muhammad, which we call the sunnah from the collection of hadith. He gave that to us in a way that we could comprehend and understand.

Some people, it was reported, thought that the transition was not taking place fast enough. As a result, confusion with respect to the direction of the organization's future was imminent. The years in Newark following the death of the honorable Elijah Muhammad witnessed at least two changes in the leadership on South Orange Avenue prior to that of the late Imam Ali K. Muslim. The expansion of the Islamic influence to other parts of the Greater Newark area in subsequent years resulted steadily from some people's inability or unwillingness to continue their support for the way the transition was being handled by the administration of the parent organization. Although some such as Imam Abdul Kareem Muhammad have interpreted the transition as being a relatively smooth one, there were others who had a different take on it. It is useful once again to quote Burhani, who stated:

> With the death and passing of Elijah Muhammad, there were a lot of people grappling with what was to come or what may come out of the new ideas, philosophy and message that Imam Warith Deen Muhammad was preaching at that time. There were a lot of people not certain of the direction they were going in. It was like going in one direction for so long, and then being turned around and taken off that path, you know . . . and then there were efforts to assimilate the old and the new, and many people became somewhat handicapped by that, I would say. They didn't understand how to bridge the gap between the old and the new. It became very difficult to do that for many people.[54]

Thus, as the 1980s approached, more and more members of the Newark branch of the Nation of Islam became interested in learning about Sunni Islam. Burhani's testimony is a case in point. He states:

> When I became a part of the so-called Nation of Islam I happened to have had an interest in the religion of Islam beyond what was being taught at that particular time. Because I was a kid of the sixties, if you will, who was searching for his roots—in doing so—I used to do a lot of reading about Islam in other places . . . on other continents . . . I knew and understood that there was more to Islam than what was being preached in terms of the social message and the nationalistic message . . . and so I wanted to learn more about what wasn't being taught beyond As Salaamu Alaikum . . . Just the words As Salaamu Alaikum was enough for me to know that we should be studying more about Islam because these words were a part of the Arabic language.[55]

In fact Burhani, a key player in the NOI transition from the old teachings to the new, was one of the people who used to study and teach Arabic even at a time when most NOI members weren't very much interested in it. He was the Arabic instructor in what was at that time called the University of Islam in the city of Newark. He taught Arabic from the kindergarten up through high school. He also taught some adults. In 1981, he and a few families broke away from the historic building known as Temple #25 located on South Orange Avenue, and established a masjid at 237 Central Avenue, East Orange, New Jersey. He was assisted by about ten to fifteen families. In reference to this, Imam Wahyudeen Shareef stated the following:

> I was a part of the group that ultimately were participants or founders of the Islamic Center of East Orange . . . I think there was a need for us to increase our influence within the area that we lived in. I think there was a need for us to increase our knowledge of what Islam was, and have that knowledge take on perhaps a fresh expression . . . I think that was the motivation. I think the motivation was more positive than anything else . . . The intent was to really establish a place that would be a reflection of the beauty and growth of Islam . . . the growth that Islam can afford people providing that they get a better understanding of how it is to be practiced, and then embracing that wholeheartedly with commitment and cooperation, and the things that can be done as a result. I think that was the spirit in which the Islamic Center of East Orange was originally established.[56]

This was a significant turning point in the history of the NOI in Greater Newark. Initially, the members who branched off remained loyal to Imam W.D. Mohammed's leadership because they understood that the Imam wanted to see the Nation of Islam evolve into something new. But, due to disagreements on the direction provided by Muslim leadership, as well as doctrinal issues and methodology, certain members of this community decided to go their separate ways. Nevertheless, the main point here is that a new page in Newark Muslim history had been written. A dawah effort, as some prefer to call it, was extended to the East Orange area. Burhani states:

In my mind, at that particular time, maybe not in other people's mind, the circumstances that I left South Orange Avenue was not really circumstances that I had any control over. My leaving South Orange Avenue was in an attempt to give people an opportunity who wanted to go further in Islam than what was being afforded to them on South Orange Avenue . . . There was an attempt, somewhat, by the individuals who were there to hold the people back if you will, or not to go ahead of the leadership then, in terms of making changes and adopting the teachings of the Qur'an and the teachings of the Prophet Muhammad or practicing the Sunnah, if you will. Some people were reluctant because they didn't know what their responsibilities were. Out of ignorance, some people were reluctant in terms of the insecurities they had in terms of being educated enough about Islam to move forward. So I was somewhat of a person at that particular time who was ahead of his time in terms of getting people to practice the religion. And, so, I was given the alternative at that time by Imam Muhammad to go on and do whatever I wanted to do in terms of trying to do something for the cause of Islam. So I took that opportunity and I moved to East Orange to an office building on Central Avenue . . . At the time, I didn't even have a job. I borrowed a hundred and some dollars to rent the place, and the owner let me have the place on the faith that I could come up with the money in order to carry it. So it was myself, and about 10 to 15 families who decided that they would assist with the running of the organization at that time.[57]

Today, the city of East Orange has a very significant Islamic influence as a result of the seed that was planted in 1981. When Imam Muhammad visited the city of East Orange in 1984 to give a public address he publicly acknowledged Ahmed Burhani and extended the Muslim greeting to him. He stated the following. "Also to Imam Ahmed Burhani, if he's here, of East Orange, we would like to give him our greetings of As Salaam Alaikum."[58] The Nation of Islam, known in 1981 as the World Community of Islam in the West, had taken another step towards congruency with orthodox Islamic teachings. It took about forty years for the gap between the Newark chapter of the NOI and the Sunni communities that began in 1941 to bridge. Although some might argue that the bridge occurred in 1975 with the changes that Imam W.D. Mohammed brought, the fact is that the leadership of the Nation of Islam in Newark at that time, according to some, was still very much in tune with the old teachings that were instituted by Elijah. Although the tauhidic seed for charting a new course had been planted in 1975, or even sooner, by

Imam W. Deen Mohammed, by 1981 the concept of Tauhid and what it truly was had become a subject within the various communities, in Newark, that could no longer be avoided. The whole idea of Tauhid and its universal appeal had become central to transforming the thinking of not only members of the NOI in Newark, but even those Muslims who thought that they had a spiritual or intellectual advantage over the people who came through the NOI experience. Imam Shareef's comments in reference to this are instructive. He stated:

> It is difficult to say when Tauhid became firmly entrenched in the minds of the people who were a part of the NOI experience. Tauhid to me is a consciousness, the oneness of the Creator. The fixing of that in a person is personal. The fixing of that, and how that evolves in a person's consciousness to a large extent depends on that person . . . It depends on what they have experienced in their life that opens up to them the vastness and greatness of this principle. I think it depends on what Allah exposes you to . . . I think sometimes the concept of Tauhid is lost even today for some of us . . . It is one thing to [speak of it] verbally, however, it is another thing for a person to realize that this principle is broad in its definition in terms of looking at Allah as Ahad (One) and at the same time looking at the connection that everything else has in creation as unity. So that principle, I think, we are still really looking at and trying to get a better understanding of it—the essence of it and what it does for our thinking. What it does for our thinking is [help us] begin to appreciate not just the unity of Allah, but the unity of His creation and seeing the connections associated with that, and seeing that even within the diversity, there is a unity.[59]

Since 1981, others have left the parent organization on South Orange Avenue and have adopted the new teachings and methodology instituted by Imam Mohammed. It took tremendous courage to let go of the old baggage and embark on a new path. Nevertheless, today, the communities who support the leadership of Imam W.D. Mohammed, including the parent organization on South Orange Avenue, renamed Masjid Imam Ali K. Muslim have come full circle into acknowledging the superiority of the tauhidic idea.

It is no doubt that Imam W. Deen Mohammed has made an extraordinary contribution to American society, the world, and to our understanding of the role and development of Islam in American society and other parts of the globe. Imam W. Deen Mohammed's history shows that he was respected as an effective leader of leaders. His influence on Muslim thought in Newark is far-reaching and quite profound. Thus it would be appropriate to highlight some general observations of his works and accomplishments. Better than any Muslim leader in the United States of America, Imam W. Deen Mohammed has been able to explain the intricacies and complexity of race, ethnicity, class and religious denomination within the American social structure. In fact, he has consistently spoken from the point of view of the American experience, and has always demonstrated his love for not only his people, but also his country. Religion as taught by him was never used as a weapon against Western culture, or as an escape from reality or civic responsibility, but as a means to transform one's self, community and society. Almost single handedly, he transformed the Nation of Islam (NOI) from a quasi-Islamic black-nationalist organization to an organization committed to the fundamental principles of a moderate brand of Islam. This is perhaps his greatest legacy. Religion, he taught, was something that should be understood as the very business of life, and as a complete way of life. He applied this understanding and teachings to the social realities of American society and to the social realities of the African American experience using the NOI that he grew up under and inherited as his social laboratory. Many of his critics and detractors, over the years, have erroneously accused him of compromising the principles of the religion. Nevertheless he is loved by many people of all races, ethnic backgrounds, classes and religious persuasion. He has somewhere around 2.5 million followers in his Mosque Cares association, perhaps the largest following among Muslims in the United States of America.

His flock refuses to part ways with him. No Muslim American leader can claim such a following. And no African-American leader is depended upon by his followers more than Imam W. Deen Mohammed. No leader has been studied more, referenced more, cross-examined more, publicly challenged more, or publicly shown affection more than this man. Yet, he is somewhat of a quiet warrior whose good works are unknown to many in the African American community and the American community-at-large. He is without a doubt an optimist. Even those who in the past have vociferously disagreed with him have in recent years humbled themselves, and on some significant level have publicly acknowledged his contributions to a better understanding of the role Islam is to play in the country and the world. He has been awarded the prestigious honorary doctorate degree by institutions of higher learning, an honor and great accomplishment to this man who received very little formal education. He has been embraced and/or sought out for advice by such luminaries and world leaders as the Reverend Dr. Robert Schuller, the late Pope John Paul II, the Honorable Minister Louis Farrakhan, former Secretary of State Madeline Albright, the Egyptian President, Hosni Mubarak, Ms. Chira Lubich of the Focolare Movement and former United States President Bill Clinton, to name a few. Some of his activities have been representing Muslims in Oxford, England at the World Parliament of Religious Leaders for the Survival of the Earth, serving on advisory panels for religious freedom at home and abroad, and promoting interfaith understanding and world peace. That he is a man with virtually no extensive academic training from any institution of higher learning or religious academy anywhere in the world is quite remarkable. He came, as many of the local people say, from amongst the common people. And the general sentiment in Newark is such that for that reason he is so loved by the common people there. His supporters in the Greater Newark community have labored hard to represent his social and political philosophy as it evolved and continues to evolve over the years. He has been successful in canonizing a growing and widely sought after commentary of American social history as it pertains to race relations. He has stood firm in his determination to liberate not only the African American mind and spirit, but also the spirit of our nation, which he believes has great potential to nurture the best model for human excellence. He has demonstrated his patriotism to his country without compromising his faith in his religion. More often than not, he is bent on finding the good in opportunities available in the U.S., acknowledging that God's plan is supreme and that nothing happens without God's permission. His approach has been to awaken the God conscious spirit within us because he understood that to do so was to empower the human being and enrich the nation and the world. In some sense he is our Martin Luther, the 16th century German figure who liberated many Christians in his day from the dogmatism and political clutches of the conservative branch of the Catholic Church. Martin Luther's movement became known as the Protestant Reformation. This reputation of being a liberator has placed him in the category of world leaders such as Martin L. King Jr., Mahatma Ghandi, and the W.E. B. DuBois and will go down in history as one of the greatest contributions to world peace. He is the foremost native born American who has used the Holy Qur'an to assess the American condition without condemning the entire American society to hell. His faith and vision for a productive life for Muslims inspires others to believe in themselves and have a vision of their own. He has distinguished himself as one who can speak to and relate to all classes of people. He has demonstrated an ability to speak to the Pope in Rome and to the poor man in the urban ghetto, be it Newark NJ or Harlem NY. This national and international recognition would open the Imam to public scrutiny. As elsewhere, Newark at times became a test for his mettle.

His influence in Newark is as equally profound. One of his greatest contributions was his success in transforming the Nation of Islam into a viable Sunni Muslim association. As it seems, the Imam had plans and aspirations to transform this organization long before he got the opportunity to do so. When he inherited the responsibility to lead the Nation of Islam, he immediately but gradually dismantled the old system and proceeded to introduce the members of the Nation of Islam to ideas and concepts that were contrary to the old teachings and consistent with orthodoxy. This feat, which was no easy task, took tremendous courage, personal sacrifice, and skill to accomplish. Many of his supporters in the Newark area are very thankful for, and appreciative of, the direction and leadership that he provided, and have pledged to support his ministry throughout the country and the world. The Imam's late but timely arrival on the national and international world stage of Islamic propagation efforts has at times been misunderstood and misrepresented even by some of his most faithful supporters. That his arrival was late is not to say that his extraordinary contribution to Islam's development in America and the world should not be recognized or valued by all Muslims. It most definitely should, but it should be examined and understood in its proper historical context, which for him began in 1975. I think that Muslim Americans have much to gain from studying his teachings and views since he, like many of them, is a native-born American of African descent. Such an individual, as Imam Muhammad has demonstrated perhaps better than any Muslim American leader over the years, is in a great, perhaps the best, position to influence the public at-large and articulate the needs, feelings and aspirations of Muslim Americans. Yet, be that as it may, gaining support from the various Muslim constituents in the Greater Newark Area has not altogether materialized for Imam Muhammad. This includes African American constituents who were former members of the Nation of Islam. Many have openly and rather disparagingly challenged the effectiveness of the Imam's ideas and choices relative to the direction that the Muslim community has taken since his rise to prominence. Some have gone so far as to question the Imam's aqeedah (belief), castigating him as a deviant because of his alleged unorthodox views relevant to the needs of native born Muslims of America, his apparent popularity among government and international figures, his moderate approach to propagating the faith, and his defense of his father's legacy. Others have expressed an appreciation of his ability and determination to use diplomacy in bridging the gap between Islam and the West. While these attitudes concerning the role of an effective Muslim leader are at the center of the controversy among African American Muslims, the bright side of it all is that there has been an apparent tolerance for other points of view. For the past twenty-five or more years all Muslims in the Greater Newark area have been welcomed at any masjid at the times of the five daily salats (prayers), the juma'ah (Friday congregational prayer), and lectures open to the public. Further, although there are still significant differences with respect to perspective, there is a growing cooperation between the various groups. To the credit of a newly emerging leadership, one that is determined to divorce itself from the old baggage of black nationalist thoughts and practices, Muslims in the Greater Newark area are beginning to understand that, while differences of opinion between human beings will always exist, agreement on the place and relevance of Tauhid in their world-view is the foundation of true unity.

Many of the former members of the Nation of Islam admit that Elijah's teachings had helped them in their personal lives; they are proud they were a part of the organization. However, there are others who came out of the same experience who in hindsight believed that it was ineffective and unnecessary to introduce African Americans to pseudo-Islamic ideas. This also lends considerable support to the claims of the older Sunni groups in the city who said from the start that Islam is based on the concept of tauhid, and that without acknowledgment of that fact no community claiming to be Muslim, truly was representative of that important Qur'anic principle. As some have observed, it is a very sensitive issue and one that is worthy of our attention and discussion. It is useful once again to quote Imam Shareef whose thoughts are representative of many who came to Islam through the experience of the NOI.

> There was much that I learned in the NOI that I had to unlearn, that is true. There was much that I learned that I ended up abandoning. There was much I learned that perhaps even became obstructions for my growth and development. That's on one hand. On the other hand, there is much that I experienced and learned in the NOI that I would not sacrifice for any experience. There is much I learned in terms of an internal discipline for myself, and I think for others, that enabled us to get in touch with our abilities to achieve. The NOI was an achieving force in the American society . . . You saw African American people making strides socially, economically and culturally that to this day, I think, is difficult to replicate. I think the NOI was able to achieve things because of this sense of commitment and belief in a mission, and the other component of this was the willingness of [people] to serve. Those lessons are priceless. You can't put a price on a person learning the lesson of commitment, learning the lesson of self-sacrifice. Now the question is did the people who went through that experience — did they go through it for naught, or were they able to take that experience and now transform it into a positive experience that now takes them to the next level, which is the presence of Islam as it is in accord with the Qur'an and the life example of Prophet Muhammad (saw)? To be able to take all those good things that happened in the NOI and galvanize those good things, and now move that into the practice of Islam . . . as understood in the Qur'an and the life example of the Prophet, those persons [involved in that movement] become greater contributors to the universality of Islam. [Why?] Because they learned some valuable lessons about sacrifice and service, and that's what Islam is about. [Allah says in the Qur'an], I have created you only to serve Me. So you take the past lesson learned about service and now you put it towards the service of Allah.[60]

Attorney Kenneth Hall, a public personality and respected voice in Greater Newark stated the following in regards to this:

The fact that many people came [to al-Islam] through the [experience of the] Nation of Islam speaks for itself as to its (NOI) importance to the development of Islam in this country. We as Afro-American people have to deal with the historic reality [of our condition]. We can not get away from it; there was oppression and racial discrimination here and that had to be addressed. So I would say even though in terms of the Islamic practices that we know were absent in the NOI, the net result is that Allah (swt) guides those to his true religion who sincerely seek to follow and seek to find guidance. I think to the extent that the NOI at least said they were Muslims took courage since it was no easy task to even identify with Islam for many people in the 30s, 40s, 50s and 60s. [It represented] a certain type of defiance that benefited Muslims everywhere. It benefited Afro-Americans in this country because some of the things that the NOI represented—the cleanliness, the do-for self attitude, the pride—all benefited not only Muslims who were not in the Nation, but it benefited Afro-Americans in general.[61]

The dialogue that exists between the Nation of Islam and the Sunni Muslims is described in Dr. Aminah Beverly McCloud's study, *African American Islam*, as a struggle between two prominent views or notions in the African American Muslim community. She states,

these are the notions of asabiya and ummah. 'Asabiya (group identity) designates a key theme in the history of African American Islam—namely, the theme of nation-building . . . African American Islam can be viewed as the history of a people attempting to create 'asabiya in a hostile environment . . .' 'Ummah in Qur'anic usage refers to the community of believers who struggle in unison to submit their will to the Will of Allah . . .' 'In this sense, the ummah is composed of many particular groups who can put aside their individual identities and mutual suspicions in order to uphold what is right, forbid injustice and worship Allah in congregation.' 'Ummah is a more general concept than 'asabiya, unifying Muslims across specific national, ethnic, and cultural boundaries.' In contemporary Islamic discourse, this idea of ummah has been cast as something that is basically opposed to 'asabiya, such that a person or community must decide whether to make its priority the formation of asabiya or the experience of ummah. Understanding the tension between these two concepts is crucial to understanding the nature and development of African American Islam in the twentieth century.[62]

The history of the Muslim community in Greater Newark in many ways has been a reflection of this tension that McCloud describes. The NOI in the 20th century represented the notion of asabiya—the desire to strengthen group affiliations among black people using religion as a means to achieve its goal. The African American Sunni community, on the other hand, best represented the notion of ummah as it rejected, though not totally, the idea of asabiya in order to remain loyal to its understanding of the concept of Tauhid.

These dynamics were seldom understood or considered by many of the foreign born Muslims who settled in Newark and developed close relationships with the Muslim African-American community beginning in the mid 1970s. Although immigrant perceptions of the indigenous Muslim community has shifted to a more positive one in recent years, negative attitudes concerning the indigenous Muslims of Newark were shaped in part by the ignorance of those who settled there, but did not know about, care to acknowledge or know what to make of the indigenous community's long history of struggle in the city. Regardless of the historical tensions that clearly existed between the various indigenous groups, the foundation for Muslim community development in the city had been laid.

FIRST ISLAMIC CONFERENCE OF
NORTH AMERICA: HELD IN NEWARK, NJ

By the time of the convening of what was termed the First Islamic Conference of North America sponsored by the Muslim World League (Rabitat al-Alam al Islami), which took place in Newark, NJ in 1977, the indigenous Muslims in that city had already established for itself a strong public presence and a foundation for further development of the growing Muslim community. This Newark conference, described by its organizers as the first of its kind, had a very strong immigrant influence and was well attended by delegates of 169 Muslim organizations, centers, mosques, institutions and societies from all over the United States and Canada.[63] Imam W. Deen Muhammad, an American born citizen, was one of the invited speakers. His remarks generally covered the historic role of the indigenous Muslim community, but more specifically the NOI experience. He also expressed his desire to strengthen Muslim unity. Also in attendance were several Muslim dignitaries from overseas such as I.S. Djermakoye, H.E. Shaikh Muhammad Ali al-Harakan, Secretary-General of the Muslim World League; H.E. Mr. Qasim Zuhairi, Deputy Secretary-General of the Islamic Conference Secretariat, Jeddah; H.E. Mr. Salem Azzam, Secretary-General of Islamic Coordinating Council of Europe; and H.E. Mr. Mustapha Cisse, Chairman of the Executive Committee of the Islamic Coordinating Council of Africa. A number of representatives of Muslim countries and high-ranking officials of the United Nations were also present at various sections and functions of the Conference. The Conference organizers also extended a special thanks to H.E. Mr. Brendon Byrne, the Governor of the State of NJ at that time and Mr. Kenneth Gibson, the Mayor of the City of Newark for their attendance.[64]

The proceedings of the Conference reveal that there were some concerns that the organizers had about the efforts and qualifications of local Muslims to propagate Islam in North America properly. One dignitary stated that "challenge comes from the fact that, firstly, local Muslims for a long time lacked Islamic education, organization and the dedicated leadership that could maintain a viable Muslim community, and secondly, the socio-cultural context in which the Muslims have to live is alien to their values, traditions and spiritual concepts."[65] These concerns, it seems, took precedence over understanding the history of North American Muslims and their encounter with white racism and anti-Islamism. And virtually no Muslim dignitary articulated or even acknowledged the over sixty-year history of efforts by the locals to establish Muslim community development. In reference to this lack of documentation of indigenous efforts, researchers such as Dr. Clement Price would also comment that even black Christians, at least during the first half of the twentieth century, accorded Muslims in Newark a kind of invisibility.

NOTES

1. Amiri Baraka, *The Autobiography of Amiri Baraka/LeRoi Jones*.

2. Khalid Ismail, interview by author, Newark, NJ January, 1998.

3. *Qur'an* 5:8.

4. *Qur'an*.

5. Matina Ismail, Interview by author, Newark, NJ 25 April 1998.

6. The term *halal* is referred to here in its religious context. As was mentioned, Muslims are instructed by Allah (God) to consume only that which is lawful. "He hath forbidden you dead meat, and blood, and the flesh of swine, and that on which any other name hath been invoked besides that of Allah. But if one is forced by necessity, without willful disobedience, nor transgressing due limits,—Then he is guiltless. For Allah is Oft-Forgiving, Most Merciful." Qur'an 2:173.

7. Aminah Beverly McCloud, *African American Islam*, (New York: Routledge, 1995), 5.

8. Robert Dannin, *Black Pilgrimage to Islam*, (New York: Oxford University Press, 2002), 5.

9. Aminah Beverly McCloud, "African American Muslim Women," in *The Muslims of America*, ed. Yvonne Yazbeck Haddad, (New York : Oxford University Press, 1991), 177.

10. McCloud, "African-American Muslim Woman."

11. Akbar Muhammad, "Muslims in the United States: An Overview of Organizations, Doctrines, and Problems," in *The Islamic Impact*, eds., Yvonne Yazbeck Haddad, Byron Haines, Ellison Findly (Syracuse, New York: Syracuse University Press, 1984), 195.

12. Matina Ismail, Interview, April 98.

13. For an excellent discussion on the evolution of Islam in America and how religious authority in the U.S. became legitimized, read Dr. Sherman A. Jackson's book, *Islam and the Blackamerican: Looking toward the Third Resurrection* published by Oxford University Press. Jackson's book is seminal and, in my judgment, he is one of the most important Muslim voices of the new millennium.

14. Khalida Haqq, Interview by the author, Newark, NJ, 25 April 1998.

15. Abdul Wali, Khalid Ismail, and Abdul-Aleem Razzaq, Interview by author, March 1997. The Baitul Quraish social and welfare system was set up in such a way to accommodate singles as well as married couples. Lodging in what was called the barracks was made available primarily to people who were not married, newcomers, families in need, and people who wanted to prove their worthiness to be apart of the community. Thus, Islamic conformity was at times difficult to enforce, but a priority of the Baitul Quraish leadership.

16. Abdullah Yasin, *Islamicizing America*, (Nashville, Tennessee: James C. Winston Publishing Co. Inc., 1996), 26–27.

17. Abdul Wali, Khalid Ismail, and Abdul-Aleem Razzaq "Interview," January 98.

18. Ahmed Batemon, Interview by author, Newark, NJ, 24 August 1997.

19. Batemon, interview.

20. Batemon, interview.

21. Jaaber, Interview, Elizabeth, NJ, June 1997.

22. Ibn Khaldun's writings have been held in the highest esteem by many world renowned scholars. Among them are Arnold Toynbee who described his book, The *Muqaddimah*, as the greatest work of its kind that has ever been created by any mind in any time or place . . . the most comprehensive and illuminating analysis of how human affairs work that has been made anywhere. Joseph Tainter, historian and anthropologist described him as the great Arab historian who developed a cyclical theory of history. E. Jefferson Murphy, author of African Civilization, characterized Khaldun as a great Islamic Historian.

23. Wahab Arbubakar, "Interview," Newark, NJ, 22 November 1997.

24. Malik Arbubakar, "Interview," Newark, NJ, 2 November 1997.

25. Malik Arbubakar, "Interview," Newark, NJ, 30 November 1997.

26. Malik Arbubakar Interview.

27. *Kerner Report*, 59.

28. *Kerner Report*. 1–2.

29. *Kerner Report*. xiii.

30. Ahmed Burhani, Interview by author, East Orange, NJ. September 1997.

31. Yusef Shakoor, Interview by author, Elizabeth, NJ, January 9, 2000.

32. Shakoor, interview.

33. Shakoor, interview.

34. Shakoor, interview.

35. Shakoor, interview.

36. Statement made by Imam James Ibn Shabazz at a public address in Newark concerning his father's legacy in Newark on February 8th 2002.

37. See *Star Ledger* article of November 14th 2002. Newark This Week, "New School will honor James Shabazz" by Barbara Kukla.

38. *Star Ledger*, November 14.

39. See Kenneth Oreilly‚s book, *Racial Matters*.

40. Steven Barboza, *American Jihad: Islam after Malcolm X*, (New York: Image, Doubleday, 1994), 15. Murad Muhammad's article, "Black Devils," provides a rare insight into the conditions and mentality that existed in the NOI at the time that Malik Shabazz was murdered.

41. *Star Ledger*.

42. *Star Ledger*.

43. Cynthia S'Thembile West, "Revisiting Female Activism in the 1960s: The Newark Branch Nation of Islam," *The Black Scholar*, Volume 26, No. 3–4, 41–48.This is an excellent source, scholarly, written from a woman's perspective.

44. West, 42.

45. West, 42.

46. West.

47. West.

48. West.

49. West.

50. West.

51. Issues concerning Islamic jurisprudence.

52. Imam Abdul-Kareem Muhammad, Interview by the author, Newark, NJ, October 1998.

53. Abdul-Kareem Muhammad, interview.

54. Burhani, Interview.

55. Burhani, Interview.

56. Imam W. Deen Shareef, interview by author, Irvington, NJ, January 17, 1999.

57. Burhani, Interview.

58. WARIS Associates, "The Door of Decision: Imam W. D. Mohammed at East Orange High School in East Orange, NJ," Lecture Series I, March 3, 1984.

59. Shareef Inteview.

60. Shareef interview.

61. Kenneth Hall, "Interview by author."

62. Aminah McCloud, *African American Islam*, 4–5.

63. This information was accessed from the *Proceedings of the First Islamic Conference in North America* housed at the Library of Congress.

64. *Proceedings of First Islamic Conference*.

65. *Proceedings of First Islamic Conference*.

Chapter Seven

Growing Pains

THE SEARCH FOR AND PRESERVATION
OF TAUHIDIC KNOWLEDGE

Historically, the leaders of the Sunni community rejected black-nationalism and have argued from the outset that al-Islam is based on the concept of *tauhid*, and that there can be no hope for a healthy and lasting Muslim community development without acknowledgment of that. At a New Jersey Islamic Convention in the 1990s, hosted by the WARIS Cultural Research and Development Center, Dr. Sulayman Nyang stated that "first of all to understand Islam's social order is to know that its creed is nonracial, universal and metaphysical and that it is based on the concept of *tauhid*. Nyang was echoing the sentiments of the late Palestinian scholar Dr. Isma'il Faruqui who stated in his comprehensive study, *Al Tawhid:*[1] *Its Implications for Thought and Life*, "traditionally and simply expressed, al tawhid is the conviction and witnessing that 'there is no god but God.'" Faruqui goes on to say that "this brief statement carries the greatest and richest meanings in the whole of Islam."[2]

Since 1941 Muslims in the Newark area, under the leadership of Muhammad Ezaldeen, have tried to live their lives in accordance with this idea, and have organized and committed themselves to conveying the meaning of *tauhid* as they understand it. It has not been until recent times that Muslims in Newark have come to understand and appreciate the sacrifices made by Ezaldeen, Jaaber, Arbubakar, Wadud and the small community of Muslims who received their Islamic training through the AAUAA. These pioneers laid the foundation in Newark for a more universal and inclusive study of Islam. Their perspective was more consistent with that of Muslims who studied and believed in the *sunnah* (the Prophet Muhammad's example and way). When one compares the AAUAA's religious studies program to that of the MSTA and the NOI, one will find beyond a shadow of a doubt that the AAUAA, comparatively speaking, depended less on the Bible and more on the Qur'an; less on the lessons acquired from studying the life of Jesus, and more on the lessons acquired from studying the life of all of the Prophets, especially Muhammad, the last Prophet according to Islam. This reality was the essential difference. However, the AAUAA was in solidarity with the MSTA and the NOI in rejecting the idea of the Trinity, although the latter developed a concept in its philosophy which was very similar to the Trinitarian doctrine of many Christians. From the AAUAA's point of view, belief in the Trinity and similar concepts was inconsistent with Islamic jurisprudence, and fell into the category of shirk (joining other gods with God). Such a charge, according to the Sunnis, was an unforgivable sin. This point of view was shaped by a direct passage from the Qur'an which states:

Allah forgiveth not (the sin of) joining other gods with him; but he forgiveth whom he pleaseth other sins than this; one who joins other gods with Allah, have strayed far, far away (from the Right).[3]

The internalization of this verse by Muslims would sometimes draw a wedge between the camps. The Sunnis would interpret the verse as meaning that the NOI's teachings were not in compliance with the *ayat* (sign). And the NOI's determination to maintain their unity of purpose in alleviating the oppressive conditions of African-Americans took precedence over the concerns of the Sunnis. Unity would sometimes be curtailed because of this, but as Muslims over time became more knowledgeable about the principles of the religion, tolerance for differences and their common struggle became their ally. Kenneth Hall stated the following in reference to this:

We used to hear frequently from brothers who were not indigenous to America. Those brothers from other places would say something that was very significant. They would say, brothers, those (meaning people who had not accepted Sunni Islam) are your brothers; those are your people; those are your family members, so you have to give them the dawah. You have to reach out to them because you are even closer to them than we are. They are your people, your tribe and we understand that. So, many of us learned from that.[4]

Although the AAUAA received very little support from foreign-born Muslims, through Ezaldeen they were in regular contact with many of them. As the African American community's first Imam, Ezaldeen would represent his constituency at Islamic conventions throughout the tri-state area. In fact,

"unity among Muslims, and collective striving, always was of great impor-
tance to Muhammad Ezaldeen."[5] "His leadership led to the formation of the
Uniting Islamic Societies of America, which subsequently held conferences
from 1943 to 1946, for the explicit purpose of uniting Muslims in America."[6]
"This effort is significant because it brought together luminaries and other
committed Islamic leaders of those times, including Wali Akram of the First
Cleveland Mosque in Ohio, Shaykh Dawud Faisal of the Islamic Mission of
America in New York, and many others."[7] The efforts of all of these individuals have been successful in bringing people into the Islamic fold. One could
reasonably argue that, although Noble Drew Ali espoused ideas of nationalism, he had a fairly good understanding of the concept of *tauhid*. That he espoused ideas which excluded European Americans from having any meaningful relationship with God during the early part of this century is well
known in the African American Muslim community. But, this had more to do
with the socio-political and socio-economic realities and conditions of which
members of his community and other African Americans faced, and thus is a
point of view that deserves more attention than scholars have given. Nevertheless, it is a point of view or an analysis which was representative of the
feelings of some downtrodden Americans. This is a fact that should not be
misunderstood by Americans, especially Muslim Americans. In fact, Noble
Drew Ali, by openly declaring himself as a "Moslem" in 1913, in many significant ways, went against the grain of the conventional wisdom of his day
and challenged the very essence of the American social system. True, the evidence clearly indicates that he did not preach a pure form of *tauhid* for lack
of a better phrase, but he did challenge the conventional wisdom of his day
about the nature of God and how God is to be viewed and understood. This
was a significant turning point for African American religion.

It should be remembered that the followers of Noble Drew Ali declared
themselves as Moorish Americans. And to be a Moorish American literally
meant that you were one committed to living a law abiding clean life and de-
voted to the cause of God. It meant that you had to learn to identify culturally
with the land and people of Morocco, while also respecting the fact that you
were born an American. Thus, it is essential to know that the Moorish Americans believed that they were a part of the larger Muslim world. The main
thing that tied them to the Muslim world, in a religious doctrinal sense, was
their rejection of the Trinitarian concept of God (three Gods in One) espoused
by most African American Christians, and their espousal of the idea that there
is no god but God who is one and alone. Although initiated by a heterodox
group, this orthodox Islamic influence predated the influences of all Muslim
groups in the Newark area today.

ISLAM COURTS JAZZ

Ahmed Batemon, a native Newarker spoke of the influence that Islam had on the jazz world. During the 1940s and 50s he witnessed the marriage of Islam and many prominent jazz musicians. For Batemon, the Islamic experience began back in 1947. His attraction to the faith was in part a result of the publicity that the religion was receiving through the conversion of many of the jazz musicians, many of whom he knew personally. Batemon's testimony provides some insight.

My Islamic experience began in 1947. Islam became more or less . . . a public thing. I know that prior to my introduction to it we had a Professor Ezaldeen on Prince Street who I later found out had actually founded a village somewhere in South Jersey called Ezaldeen Village. But my first introduction to Islam was through Muhammad Sadiq who was formerly called Howard Scott, a trombonist with Billy Eckstine's orchestra. Muhammad Sadiq and Marion Sadiq who lived down on Barkley Street in Newark, I met them through a bunch of aspiring musicians . . . Through them I went to a debate at the Hotel Diplomat sometime in 1947. The debate was between Sir Muhammad Zakara Khan of the Ahmadiyyah movement and Dr. Muhammad Sidiki who was a Sufi . . . The Ahmadis had a mission at 115 West 116th street, up above a pawn shop, right off Lenox Avenue, and the missionary there was B. Yasin. And there I met a lot of Muslim musicians, mostly New York people. I met Abdul Burhani which was Art Blakey, Saeed Shahab who was Edmond Gregory, a saxophone player, Talib Dawud who was Barrymore Rainy, a trumpet player. I also met Aleem Rasheed who I think was a trumbone player. They were all Ahmadi Muslims. They formed a Muslim band, a large number of Muslim musicians. I became involved with them. Actually, my first interest in Islam came after reading a book called the teachings of Islam by Ghulam Ahmed who was a man who claimed to be the promised Messiah and the Mahdi from the Punjab in what's now known as Pakistan. At the time, I was still in school, and lived on the South Side and after school I would go to Sadiq's to learn the Salat. This was in 1947 because I graduated from Southside (now Malcom X Shabazz Highshool in Newark) in 1949.[8]

In 1953, Ebony Magazine did a story on Muslim musicians. The title of the article was "Moslem Musicians, Mohammedan religion has great appeal for many talented progressive jazz men." The article states:

There are today a large number of Negro Americans who have embraced the Moslem faith. They perform the daily prayer ritual, observe the dietary laws laid down by the Prophet and each sun-down turn their faces toward Mecca. Slightly more than 200 of this number are jazz musicians, mostly on the modern kick.

The American Negroes who have rejected Christianity for the Moslem way have explanations for their conversion that cover a wide range of spiritual, personal and emotional factors. There is among the Negro Moslems here a unity of thought on one point: Islam breaks down racial barriers and endows its followers with purpose and dignity.[9]

Ebony magazine reports that "in 1947 a group of New York musicians headed by brilliant base drummer Art Blakey and bop trumpeter Barrymore Rainey organized a Moslem mission which met in Blakey's Harlem apartment until they outgrew the space."[10] Within six years the group increased to over 100 members which made it necessary to relocate to a larger site. Blakey was reported to have said, "Islam has made me feel more like a man, really free."[11] Also, "Ahmad Jamal, a famous pianist who was also among this bunch, was reported to have accepted Islam in 1951."[12] During the Ebony interview he stated "Islam has given me a spiritual peace."

Perhaps most useful to this study is the part of Ebony's coverage of the life of Lynn Hope, a popular saxophonist who was reported to have been a fluent Arabic reader and speaker, and the head of a Philadelphia Moslem group called the Universal Arabic Association.[13] Hope was said to have worked as a hospital orderly in Newark while he furthered his Islamic studies. In an interview he stated:

Islam altered my entire life and gave me a new personality. Islam changed my life completely. It gave me a new outlook on life and assured my success. I have learned how to treat my fellow men with justice and how to conduct my business efficiently and honestly. Islam gave me spiritual peace and mental satisfaction. I now get more joy out of playing my saxophone, and is able to work much harder.[14]

"He used Qur'an principles to guide him in negotiating contracts, making bookings and determining salaries of members of his band."[15] Ebony went on to say that "Hope avidly propagated his faith among all kinds of Americans."[16] He believed that more Americans should become Moslems because Islam recognizes no race or color distinctions. A philosophy such as Islam, he felt, was best for America because it would wipe out white supremacy and elevate the Negro to equality. This idealism was the general feeling of most that became a part of the group. These Muslims were concerned with the right to follow one's conscience and the right of the individual to choose, but they were also very much interested in improving the living conditions of black people. To be a part of the group was predicated upon the willingness of an individual, at least in principle, to accept all people as human beings on equal footing as opposed to a member of any particular race. To maintain this universal idealism was often very difficult due to the stubborn attitudes of many conservative whites and their resistance to social change, a point often made by those who followed the path of black-nationalism.

ARAB, MUSLIM AND BLACK

Richard Brent Turner in his informative book *Islam in the African American Experience* stated, "as the 1950s progressed, gradually a split occurred in the Indian Ahmadiyyah[17] movement as many black people passed through its ranks because they became disenchanted with its multi-racial agenda . . ."[18] "Turner says that some of these African Americans went to Sunni groups because by doing so they believed that they could Arabize their identities to escape the stigma attached to blackness.[19] Be that as it may, there is some clarity that should be brought to this issue. Most who joined the African American Sunnis learned the important lesson that the term Arab was a linguistic term and not a racial one. The Hametics under Ezaldeen's influence were taught this lesson. Although they were taught that the original Arabs were Black or at least a non-white people whose original tongue was Arabic, the emphasis in their teachings was placed on language, not race, as the highest form of identification for a person. Race is a social construct that was created by Europeans of the modern era; it had nothing to do with culture. Language, on the other hand, the Sunnis taught, was inextricably tied to culture, which is why so much emphasis by them historically has been placed on learning the Arabic language. So for them an Arab was one who spoke the Arabic language and not someone who had particular skin pigmentation. Their perspective and vision with regard to hopes of mastering the Arabic language, it seems, was consistent with that of the Muslims during the classical Islamic period. The Prophet Muhammad is quoted to have said one who speaks Arabic is an Arab. The Prophet Muhammad also said in his last sermon that "an Arab is no better than a non-Arab and a non-Arab is no better than an Arab, a black is no better than a white and a white is no better than a black, the best of you in the sight of God is the one who is the most righteous."[20] Hence, the criterion for being a true Muslim as taught by the Prophet Muhammad had nothing to do with one's ability to speak Arabic. To be a true Muslim all one had to do was to take the *Shahadatain* (a public declaration bearing witness that there was only one God with Muhammad ibn Abdullah as His messenger) and live to the best of their ability in accordance with the spirit of the Qur'an and Sunnah.

CHARTING A NEW COURSE:
ON BEING MUSLIM, AMERICAN AND PATRIOT

"Others [like the celebrated Muhammad Ali] joined the Nation of Islam because they were attracted to its black-nationalist agenda [and its display of
brotherhood and power among black people.]"[21] The struggle between these
two paths (black-nationalist and Sunni) are more often than not discussed
within the context of Western paradigms of thought and seldom discussed
within an Islamic ideological framework. Those who were attracted to the Islamic religion in the late nineteenth century and the first half of the twentieth
century and became leaders of their people sought to change that. Like the
men of the Age of Enlightenment in Europe in the 15th and 16th centuries, it
was Muslim personalities such as Mohammed Alexander Russell Webb, Noble Drew Ali, W. D. Farad, Elijah Muhammad and Muhammad Ezaldeen who
were in search of a new intellectual tradition or, as theologian James Cone
might say, a liberation theology that endeavored to chart a new course for
their people and the oppressed masses in the twentieth century. To participate
in the efforts of charting this new course for their people and a country in
search of the greatest good for the greatest number of people has been the
quest of the most informed and learned among Muslim Americans. The
Prophet Muhammad, the leader of all Muslims, is purported to have re-intro-
duced to the Arab world in the 7th century A.D. a kind of teaching that ap-
pealed to the intellect and the soul of the human being. This teaching was ap-
plicable across time and space. It was said to be the liberation theology of not
only Prophet Muhammad's day, but of all times and within the reach of every
person who was willing to surrender their will to the Will of the Creator.
Thus, there was no contradiction between having faith in al-Islam and feeling
love for all people and one's country. If to be patriotic means to show love,
devotion and loyalty to the best and highest principles of one's country, in
time, history will bear witness to the patriotism of Muslim Americans. For
certain, it is this spirit of patriotism that has been and continues to be evident
in the teachings of the American born national Muslim leader, Imam W. Deen
Mohammed, whose influence in Newark, NJ since 1975 has instilled in his
followers pride, confidence and a strong sense of civic responsibility. As history attest, participation in the American political process has not always been
an objective of the former members of the old Nation of Islam. But, with the
help of the teachings of Imam W. Deen Mohammed, the leadership of the
Muslim community in Greater Newark has shifted its focus to become more
involved in the day to day workings of the American democracy. This position of the Imam, it seems to me, was not taken as a result of political expe-
diency, but rather as a result of his principled belief in the integrity of the

American political process and, more importantly, his confidence in the power of God-conscious men and women of all faiths to use their influence to serve their country and the American people on all levels. "We are not enjoying the [benefits] of this democracy to an appreciable extent," the Imam stated at a public lecture in East Orange on March 3, 1984. Building on the foundation laid by his father, Imam Mohammed invested energy in preparing the Imams, leaders and public servants in support of his ministry for responsibility and leadership in American civic life. Among the many who has risen to prominence in leadership capacities in Greater Newark is Mayor Wayne Smith of Irvington, Councilman D. Bilal Beasely, the late Imam Ali K. Muslim of Masjid Mohammed, Imam Akbar Muhammad of Masjid Ali K. Muslim, Imam Wahyuddeen Shareef of Masjid Warith-id Deen, Imam Abdul Kareem Muhammad of Masjid Al-Haqq-Newark, Imam Aqeel Mateen of United Muslim Inc., Imam Abdul Aleem Razzaqq, chaplain intern at University of Medicine and Dentistry of NJ, and many others. In addition to those listed above, the Imam's teachings have inspired countless others in this state and across the nation, this writer included, and have truly empowered the common Muslim

Newark's Masjid Al-Haqq Assistant Imam Abdul-Aleem Razzaqq (far left), intern chaplain at the University of Medicine and Dentistry of New Jersey (UMDNJ) and liaison between the Greater Newark Muslim Community and the University Hospital, poses for a picture after a presentation on "Islam and Bioethics" at UMDNJ organized and facilitated by local Muslim leaders and the Hospital's Pastoral Care Committee. (Photo by Author.)

in these United States of America to accept the challenge and responsibility of becoming actors rather than spectators in the affairs of humans.

UNCOVERING THE STORIES/CONTINUING THE PROGRESS

Anna Bustill-Smith in *Reminiscences of Colored People of Princeton NJ,* copyrighted in 1913, stated "there are so few histories of colored people, so few records of their brave and honorable deeds in history that I feel constrained to record a few facts relative to these people." The same for me holds true about the Muslim pioneers in Newark. Newark, although historians did not acknowledge it, became in the early twentieth century a place of settlement for Muslims who contributed to and enriched its urban culture. The account here is only a cursory glance of their efforts and achievements in that city. Indeed, this research shows that Newark was also a springboard for the organization of Muslim communities among African-Americans. As to why Newark became this place that would welcome the Islamic influence is not a very difficult thing to understand. For one, the search for liberty in Newark had a long history since it was in New Jersey, one of the original thirteen colonies. Secondly, when one takes the time to reflect on what the goals and spirit of the American Revolution was and the historic role that Newark played in achieving it, it comes as no surprise that people of the Islamic faith would eventually be welcomed there. Muslims like many others in search of freedom became attracted to the city of opportunity in the early part of the twentieth century and were determined to carve out a space for themselves. While they struggled to gain acceptance, they, over time, were able to make the struggle of establishing Islam in America an important part of the American saga. Kenneth Hall stated:

I think Newark's long history of activity of being in the forefront on a lot of social levels makes it unique among cites. Newark, I think is the third oldest city in the country. If we look at the early Islamic-influenced movements that we know particularly affected the Afro-American community; they had their origins in Newark. Some of the principal people were Noble Drew Ali and Muhammad Ezaldeen. If you look at the early 1970s, the efforts by Imamu Amiri Baraka and his organization—Committee for a Unified Newark—and the effect that that organization had on the whole nationalist movement of the 1960s when Imamu was the chief organizer of the political convention in Gary, he was from Newark, as a result, Newark's presence was felt in that type of liberating organization back then. In fact, the first meeting back in 1969 or 1970, Baraka was very instrumental in organizing that effort and pioneering it through that period. His constituency was people from Newark. And many of those people who were in with the Committee for a Unified Newark are Muslims today. And he, Imamu, is reported to have taken Shahada himself even though he did not continue to practice Islam. But, that is the influence of Newark. So if you look back, Islam was very prevalent here in Newark and the influence of it has been felt. Many of the leaders that have achieved national and international recognition, who have impacted the lives of the people have been Muslims or connected to some kind of Muslim influence. To that extent, Newark is a very key place because Islamic love and sentiment and influence are here and it emanates out to other people in this country and throughout the world. And you find many people will often say that they have been to a lot of different places in the country, and they never feel the Muslim influence as they feel around the Newark area. I always recall a friend, a former Principal of the school for a few years, from Pittsburgh coming here and him being so overwhelmed with being in downtown Newark and hearing Salaam Alaikum. These greetings coming sometimes from people who were obviously out of it, down on their luck, considered bums, or winos or whatever would give them salaams. He always remembered . . . every time he comes to Newark, everyone is a Muslim. Many other people have had that type of feeling when they come to Newark. That influence going back to these organizations that pioneered the Addeynu Allahe Universal Arabic Association and the Moorish Holy Temple of Science, all of these had a kind of Islamic influence on the people and so Newark was a key place and a key city for Islam. We hope that it will continue. As Newark's Renaissance continues, we hope that the Islamic Renaissance will continue in Newark too.[22]

THE INFLUENCE OF MINISTER LOUIS FARRAKHAN

The influence of Minister Louis Farrakhan, a major Muslim leader well known to the American public, has too been felt in the city of Newark. His Million Man March, more than any event in recent American history, captured the imagination of the urban poor. Kahera stated that "until the Million Man March on October 16, 1995, the 1963 civil rights march led by Martin Luther King Jr.—which included men and women of many races and drew 250,000 people—was the most significant civil rights gathering in our nation's history that was organized by church leaders."[23] Kahera's observation, no doubt, is a very important one and underscores a shift in the emergence of a new Muslim activism in the struggle for civil rights. On that bright October day, Minister Farrakhan met with a million men as they flooded the national Mall in Washington D.C. His effort to assemble a million men on the Mall won a great deal of support from the black church. "It is reported that 875,500 people (according to the Park service) and 1.5 million people (according to the Nation of Islam) attended the Million Man March."[24] Nowhere was the spirit of the march felt greater than in the city of Newark, NJ. This unprecedented event in American history inspired the establishment of Women in

Support of the Million Man March (WISOMMM). Headquartered in Newark, WISOMMM is an organization comprised of self-made and professional black women who have pledged to do their best to help uplift the disadvantaged people in the greater Newark community. A multi-religious group led by Newark native Fredricka Bey, WISOMMM has rapidly become a leading voice for the urban poor and disadvantaged members of society as well as a defender of religious freedom.

NOTES

1. The most common variations in the transliteration of the concept among English speakers are as follows: *Tauhid, Tauheed, Tawhid, Tawheed*.

2. al Faruqi, Isma'il Raji, *Al Tawhid: Its Implications for Thought and Life*, (Herndon, Virginia: International Institute of Islamic Thought, 1992), 9.

3. Qur'an 4:48.

4. Kenneth Hall, interview by author, East Orange, NJ, 15, January 2001.

5. [Addeynu Allahe Universal Arabic Association Inc.?] Our Story, Nowhere: Nonesuch Press, 8.

6. Addeynu Allahe, Our Story.

7. Addeynu Allahe, Our Story.

8. Walter Ahmed Batemon, Interview by author, Newark, NJ, 24 August 1997.

9. "Moslem Musicians:Mohammedan religion has great appeal for many talented progressive jazz men," *Ebony*, April 1953,104–111.

10. "Moslem Musicians."

11. "Moslem Musicians."

12. "Moslem Musicians."

13. "Moslem Musicians."

14. "Moslem Musicians."

15. "Moslem Musicians."

16. "Moslem Musicians."

17. This was a proto-Islamic movement started by Muslims from India that attracted some African Americans to its ranks beginning in the 1920s. The Ahmadiyyah Movement, like the MSTA and the NOI, was generally well known for its heterodox views and practices.

18. Richard Turner, *Islam in the African American Experience*, (Bloomington and Indianapolis, Indiana, 1997), 140.

19. Turner, *Islam in the African-American Experience*, 140.

20. This is stated in the Prophet Muhammad's last sermon.

21. Prophet's last sermon.

22. Hall interview.

23. Kahera, Akel, "Urban Enclaves, Muslim Identity and the Urban Mosque in America," *Journal of Muslim Minority Affairs*, Vol. 22, No. 2, 2002, 370.

24. Kahera, "Urban Enclaves," 370.

Conclusion

Since the year 1913, many people in Greater Newark, especially those of African descent, have been influenced by the religion of Islam, the religion of Prophet Muhammad. Throughout Newark history, the people who chose to identify with Islam's culture were known by many names. First there was Noble Drew Ali's Moorish American community. Second, there were the Hametic Arabs of the Addeynu Allahe Universal Arabic Association founded by Muhammad Ezaldeen in 1938. Third, there were the Hametic Arabs of Baitul Quraish founded by Kamil Wadud in 1970. Fourth, there was the Nation of Islam, which established its first major Temple in the city in 1961, and made a transition to Sunni Islam in 1975. It was largely through the influence of these organizations that Islam became a significant part of Newark's urban culture.

A close examination of this period of history shows that the Moorish American community directly or indirectly influenced the groups that came after it. There were similarities in styles of dress, lingo, and views relative to an ancient identity. The lingo often served to distinguish these people as people of African descent who had a common history, lineage, and struggle. However, a significant difference was that, unlike the Moorish Americans, the Hametics under Ezaldeen and Wadud had a strong Sunni or orthodox orientation. Because the Hametics had internalized the concept of Tauhid many years before the members of the Nation of Islam did, they from the very beginning concentrated on teaching their members about the importance of practicing the fundamentals of Islam, more specifically the five pillars. The Nation of Islam's approach was different.

Although the Nation of Islam was active in the city since 1959, its activities were in many ways separate and very distinct from those who considered themselves Sunni. Up until 1975, its program had a black-nationalist philosophy.

115

From 1975 to 1981, the organization was adjusting to the new direction initiated by Elijah Muhammad's son, Wallace D. Muhammad. As a result of a controversy at Muhammad's Mosque #25 about how the community was to proceed with Muslim community development and Islamic propagation efforts, a group of families from the Mosque led by Ahmed Burhani moved to East Orange. As a result of this migration, today, the Sunni Muslim influence there is very strong with many Muslims working as public servants.

According to research done by the American Muslim Alliance of New Jersey there are about 400,000 Muslims in the Garden State. Although determining the number of Muslims in the state has been difficult, observers estimate that there are between 10,000 and 15,000 practicing Muslims in the Greater Newark area. Others have estimated the numbers at 20,000 to 25,000. Whatever the accurate figure is, one thing we can say for certain is that Muslims have made their presence felt in New Jersey.

This research shows that although this rapidly emerging community is diverse, and has struggled over the years to define itself, it has been steadfast in sharing its views of justice and in articulating an argument for why Islam has been attractive to African Americans. Let us be mindful that although such men as Noble Drew Ali, Muhammad Ezaldeen, Kamil Wadud, Minister James 3X Shabazz and others represented different movements at different periods of Newark Muslim history, their primary goal was basically the same—to inculcate an independent mindset and a feeling of self worth and pride among people of African descent. Indeed, this goal shows continuity within the Muslim African American experience. In the collective mind of the four leaders mentioned above, the purpose was not only to share Islam and help African Americans, but also to help in purging American society of the many social ills that seek to destroy any progressive trend towards the establishment of a true democracy devoid of racism, sexism, injustice, religious intolerance and poverty. This independent mindset and feeling of self worth, they thought, could be best brought about by recapturing a cultural legacy that was rooted in Islamic history and thought.

What is central to this study is to know that all of these individuals were pioneers, and that these pioneers of Islam in Newark left a great legacy. Although at certain points there was friction between and within the different communities, the friction seldom resulted in violence but rather expansion and/or at most a war of words. Some of the students of the earliest pioneers have produced publications and established institutions that continue to inform people about the legacy of Muslims of African descent. The identification with or longing to be in some way connected with Africa and the Kaba in Mecca suggests that, in their minds, Africa and the Kaba was considered to be important symbols for the liberation of the black mind. This also suggests that there was continuity relative to how Islam and black identity was being promulgated in the African American Muslim community and that there was a strong relationship between Islam and the continent of Africa. Historian Dr. Abdullah Hakim Quick said the following in regards to this idea:

> to be Mecca-centric yet in touch with the African world; to be an authentic Muslim yet still in touch with African-American spirituality; to be a moral person yet still in touch with the pulse of the African-American youth; to develop Islam in America without getting lost in the Muslim world.

The irony of it all is that these views had been held by people who were indigenous to these Western shores. It was, as the late Imam Muhammad Armiya NuMan stated, "wisdom from the West."

Bibliography

[Addeynu Allahe Universal Arabic Association.?] *Our Story*. Nowhere: Nonesuch Press.

al Faruqi Ismail R. *Al Tawhid: Implications for Thought and Life*. Herndon, Virginia: International Institute of Islamic Thought, 1992.

Ali, Noble Drew. *The Holy Koran of the Moorish Science Temple of America*. 1929.

Amir, Hakim. "Newark Welcomes Imam W. Deen Muhammad," *Muslim Journal* 12 No. 38, (July 1987)

Austin, Allan D. *African Muslims In Antebellum America: A source book*. New York: Garland Publishing, Inc., 1984.

Austin, Allan D. *African Muslims In Antebellum America: Transatlantic Stories and Spiritual Struggles*. New York: Routledge, 1997.

Baraka, Amiri. *The Autobiography of LeRoi Jones/Amiri Baraka*. New York, NY: Freundlich Books, 1984.

Bracey, John H., Meier, August and Rudwick, Elliot. eds. *Black Nationalism in America*. Indianapolis and New York: Bobbs-Merrill Company Inc., 1970.

Clegg, Claude Andrew. *An Original Man: The Life and Times of Elijah Muhammad*. New York: St. Martin's Press, 1997.

Cunningham, Barbara. ed. *The New Jersey Ethnic Experience*. New Jersey: Wm. H. Wise & Co., 1977.

Cunningham, John T. *Newark*. New Jersey: New Jersey Historical Society. Newark, 1966.

Dannin, Robert. *Black Pilgrimage To Islam*. New York: Oxford University Press, 2002.

Ebony. "Moslem Musicians: Mohammedan religion has great appeal for many talented progressive jazz men." April 1953. 104–111.

Farrad, Prince A. "Moorish Science History." *The Universal Truth*. 2.3 : 18–21.

Fauset, Arthur H. *Moorish Science Temple of America*. New Jersey: Universal Research Associates, 1994.

General Centre World Youngmen Muslim Association. Cairo, United Arab Republic. Atlas Press, 11,13, Souk el Tawfikia, Cairo.

Haddad, Yvonne. ed. *The Muslims of America*. New York: Oxford University Press, 1991.

Haddad, Yvonne Yazbeck & Smith, Idleman Jane. eds. *Muslim Communities In North America*. SUNY Series in Middle Eastern Studies, ed. Shahrough Akhavi, Albany: State University of New York Press, 1994.

Haddad, Yvonne Y., Haines Byron, and Ellison Findly eds. *The Islamic Impact*. Syracuse, New York: Syracuse University Press, 1984.

Hine, Darlene. *The African-American Odyssey*, volume one to 1877. Upper Saddle River, NJ: Prentice Hall, 2000.

Jaaber, Heshaam. *The Final Chapter . . . I Buried Malcolm (Hajj Malik El-Shabazz)*. Jersey City, New Jersey: New Mind Productions, 1993.

Kahera, Akel Ismail. *Deconstructing the American Mosque: Space, Gender and Aesthetics*. Austin, Texas: University of Texas Press, 2002.

Kerner Report. National Advisory Commission on Civil Disorders. New York: Pantheon Books, 1968.

Lincoln, C. Eric. *The Black Muslims In America*. Revised edition. Queens, New York: Kayode Publications, Ltd.,1973.

Martin, Tony. *Race First*. Dover, Mass.: The Majority Press, 1976.

Mazrui, Ali. *Africanity Redefined: Collected Essays of Ali Mazrui*, Vol. 1. Trenton, NJ: Africa World Press, 2002.

McCloud, Aminah B. *African American Islam*. New York: Routedge, 1995.

McCray, Walter A. *The Black Presence in the Bible*. Chicago, Illinois: Black Light Fellowship, 1990.

Muhammad, Akbar. "Some Factors which Promote & Restrict Islamization in America." *The American Journal of Islamic Studies*. 1 Num. 2 August 1984.

Muhammad, Akbar. "Interaction Between "Indigeneous" and "Immigrant" Muslims in the United States: Some Positive Trends." *Hijrah Magazine*. March/April 1985, 13–15.

Nyang, Sulayman.S. *Islam, Christianity, and African Identity*. Brattleboro, Vermont: Amana Books, 1984.

Price, Clement A. *Freedom Not Far Distant: A Documentary History of Afro-Americans in New Jersey*. Newark, NJ: New Jersey Historical Society, 1980.

Price, Clement A. "The Afro-American Community of Newark 1917–1947." Ph.D. diss., Rutgers University, 1975.

Price, Clement A. "The Beleaguered City as Promised Land: Blacks in Newark, 1917–1947. *Urban New Jersey since 1870*, ed. William C. Wright. Trenton, NJ 1974.

Quick, Abdullah H. *Islam and the African in America: The Sunni Experience*. Ontario Canada: Islamic Academy of Canada, 1997.

Rashad, Adib. *Elijah Muhammad & the Ideological Foundation of the Nation of Islam*. Hampton, Virginia: U.B.& U.S. Communications Systems, 1994.

Sabree, Hakim. "Revolution Starts in the Culture," *Muslim Journal*. 20. 10 23 December 1994.

Turner, Richard Brent. *Islam in the African American Experience*. Bloomington & Indianapolis: Indiana University Press, 1997.

Udom, Essien. *Black Nationalism: A search for an identity in America*. Chicago, Illinois: The University of Chicago Press, 1962.

Walker, Dennis. *Islam and the Search for African-American Nationhood*. Atlanta, Georgia: Clarity Press, 2005.

Wright, Giles. *Afro Americans in New Jersey*. Trenton, New Jersey: Historical Commission., 1988.

Yasin, Abdullah. *Islamizing America*. Nashville, Tennessee: James C. Winston Publishing Company, Inc., 1996.

Index